Historic Tales

of the

UPPER OHIO VALLEY

PAUL J. ZUROS

THE
History
PRESS

Published by The History Press
Charleston, SC
www.historypress.com

First published 2023

Manufactured in the United States

ISBN 9781467152983

Library of Congress Control Number: 2022949466

CONTENTS

This work is affectionately dedicated to my wife, Abigail, and our children, Paulie, Francis, Arthur and Stella.

"L'amor che move il sole e l'altre stelle." —Paradiso, *33:145*

ACKNOWLEDGEMENTS

*T*his publication would never have come to be without the constant love, support and encouragement of my dear wife, Abigail. Her devotion is selfless, and she has given so much of herself to our family. I could not ask for a more perfect love, companion and friend to walk this life with. And for all her time editing, correcting and fixing my work, this publication is very much hers as it is mine. Without her, this work would simply not have been possible. Also, thank you to my dear children, Paulie, Francis, Arthur and Stella. Their childhood innocence and unending curiosity about their world inspires me so much every day. My life would be empty without them. Thank you to my parents, Paul and Jolene Zuros, who gave so much of themselves to make me the person I am today. Without their encouragement, love and sacrifices, my career in history would not have been possible. I want to especially acknowledge my grandmother Lois Carpini for always being there to listen, guide me and champion my success. I am grateful for her love and support, which I have been blessed with throughout my life. Thank you to my late grandparents, Paul and Angela Zuros and Joseph Carpini, whose enduring memory lives on in the stories and legacy they left behind. And thank you to my sister, Cara; my brother-in-law, Chris; and my nephew, Joseph. Thank you for always being there to love, support and encourage me through so much. Thank you to my family, Joel and Debbie Carpini, Stanley and Jessica Zuros and Lillian Zuros, who have always been such an important and special part of my life. And thank you to my mother- and father-in-law, Karen and

Chris Gardner; my sister-in-law, Danielle Gardner; and my wife's cousin Matt Beideman. A heartfelt thanks to Dennis Jones, who always believed in me and contributed greatly to this work and the history of our area. Thank you to my friends at Historic Fort Steuben: Jerry and Judy Barilla, Judy Bratten, Mary Snyder, Larry Coleman, Mary Beth and Larry Bauer, Sandy Sutherland, Dave Nicholson, Dan Filbert and the Board of Historic Fort Steuben. Thank you to the late Joe and Betty Dolentin and their daughter Amy, who treated me like their own family and gave me nothing but the best. Thank you to my eighth grade West Virginia history teacher, Mrs. Terry McAtee, who inspired and encouraged me to work hard for my goals and learn all I could about our state's history. Thank you to my friends Richard Delatore, Linda and Roger Hilty, Jayne Wilson, Thom Way, Dorothy Robinson, Cathy Adam, Thomas Carpini and family, Lewis Anile, Roger Criss and the late Victor and Marjorie Greco, and thank you to my friends at the Weirton Area Museum and Cultural Center, the Hancock County Historical Museum and the Jefferson County Historical Association. Finally, to Ross Gallabrese and the *Steubenville Herald Star* and the *Weirton Daily Times* for publishing my work over the past several years— thank you!

PREFACE

*T*he place we live in is so important. It has the power to shape who we are and what we do with our future. The place I love and the place that has shaped me is the Ohio Valley. I grew up here, not during the boom years of the steel mills and factories but during the so-called deindustrialization of the main industry that sustained us for so many years. I lived on the stories of what "once was," "is gone," "was there"—and I was fascinated. What was here? Why do we do that? For what reason is this this way? Learning the stories of our community's past, I have always felt, has been the key to my understanding of who we are as a community and where we can go in the future. This place and its stories have shaped my profound love for history and this place we all call home.

My name is Paul Zuros, and I was formerly the executive director of Historic Fort Steuben in Steubenville. Before this position, I was fortunate to work for a historic house museum in Charleston, West Virginia; the West Virginia Humanities Council; and the Carnegie Museums in Pittsburgh, among other places. Having grown up here, I am connected with the Hancock County Historical Museum and the Weirton Area Museum and Cultural Center— the places that jump-started my career as a public historian.

I am an ambassador of our history. My role is, basically, to tell our stories—stories of our community and our region—and, in some cases, to share how these stories fit into our national history. It's these places and these stories that set the Ohio Valley apart—they are what makes us unique. With that in mind, I want to introduce this publication as a collection of stories of our local history, what we remember about our collective past and why it's so important. I will seek to discover and, sometimes, rediscover those stories, landmarks, events and disasters in our local history that may have been lost or forgotten. My column in the newspaper is called "History in the Hills" because the hills are just about the oldest things around here, so quite literally, our history begins in these hills.

In my role at the fort, I had the unique opportunity to connect visitors to Steubenville and the fort to the history of our area. I used the fort, as the landmark and anchor of the downtown, to set the stage for our community's past by starting with the first notable landmark in Steubenville. Although Fort Steuben supposedly disappeared from the landscape somewhere around 1790, we can still talk about this block, between Market and Adams Streets, through time and space, coming full circle to 1989, when ground was broken on the Fort Steuben reconstruction.

There is so much local history wrapped up in this particular block. There were homes here, businesses, an ice cream factory and a railroad freight station, not to mention a wharf at the end of Market Street, followed by the Market Street Bridge, which opened to traffic on July 4, 1905, the dawn of a new century. And on this block, there were parking lots, many of which took the place of landmarks that aren't there anymore. The fort is a success story about turning what was once a parking lot back into a landmark, and there are other stories that are also about overcoming obstacles to bring back important landmarks in our area—just one step in revitalizing our place in this community. History is all around us. Join me to explore our place in history in the Ohio Valley and see what we discover or rediscover along the way.

Chapter 1

OUR EARLIEST NEIGHBORS

*W*hether we realize it or not, our history is tied to the Ohio River. Flowing through our community over millennia, the river cut the Ohio Valley deeply, giving us the landscape we are all familiar with. Looking back to the earliest history of this area, we can discover that there has been human habitation here in the Ohio Valley for a long time. Not more than thirty minutes away, following Cross Creek, the Meadowcroft Rockshelter in Avella, Pennsylvania, interprets the incredible story of the discovery of an encampment that early prehistoric people used in our area. Because datable evidence was found on the floor of the shelter, archaeologists can date the earliest finds to more than nineteen thousand years ago. This is one of the oldest sites of human habitation in North America, and it's right here in our Ohio Valley.

Not quite so far back, Native Americans used the valley for hunting, gathering and living. Just right across the river from Historic Fort Steuben, high on the hill overlooking the city of Steubenville on the West Virginia side, is what is known as the East Steubenville Site. This is the location of a Native American encampment of a people who were part of what is known as the Panhandle Archaic Culture. This was primarily a group of people who drew their food from the Ohio River in the form of freshwater mussels, which they then carried up three hundred feet to the ridgetop. Many artifacts were discovered there, including six prehistoric burials, all dating this encampment back over four thousand years. If you visit Highland Hills Memorial Gardens, you can see a monument dedicated to the reinterred

Native Americans who were found at this site. Similar artifacts and mussel shells were found when excavating for the reconstruction of the fort.

During the mid-eighteenth century, the Ohio Valley was the subject of one of the very first world wars fought in history. The control of the Ohio Valley was hotly contested by the French from the North and the English from the East. The French argued that the upper Ohio River belonged to the French king, but the English fought to protect their claim of the area, as well. What resulted was a very bloody conflict known as the French and Indian War in the New World and the Seven Years' War in Europe. Battles took place from the Ohio Valley to Quebec, New York and Nova Scotia. Fighting ended in 1763 with the signing of the Treaty of Paris. After the war, the English having prevailed, taxes were imposed on the colonies to pay for the conflict. Of course, taxation without representation was one of the central grievances leading up to the American Revolution. Truly, the eyes of the world were on our valley in the 1750s and '60s.

The river was an important reason settlement came to the valley in the late eighteenth, nineteenth and twentieth centuries. The site of Fort Steuben was chosen for its vantage over the river, and the subsequent town that developed around the area was in no small part chosen for its proximity to

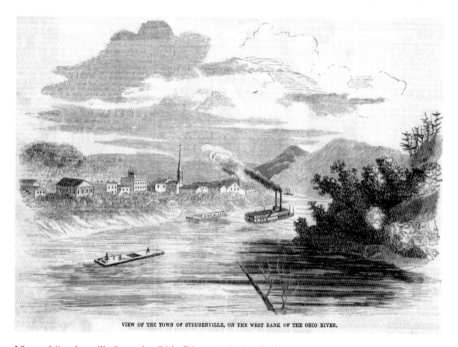

VIEW OF THE TOWN OF STEUBENVILLE, ON THE WEST BANK OF THE OHIO RIVER.

View of Steubenville from the Ohio River. *Author's collection.*

river traffic—the major highway through our region. E.T. Weir, founder of Weirton Steel, chose the community around Holliday's Cove to establish his plant after droughts brought a lack of water to their Clarksburg mill, enticing them to locate a new factory where there was a body of water that surely would not dry up. It takes a lot of water to make steel.

The river has always attracted people to this area. From prehistoric hunter-gatherers to early twentieth-century industrialists, not to mention countless settlers, statesmen, frontiersmen and immigrants, the river continues to draw travelers and impact our history. On October 22, 1770, George Washington passed by via canoe and stopped in Mingo Town, writing about his experience touring the Ohio Valley. The river was "swift" and "without shallows," according to his journal, giving him and his companions considerable difficulty on their journey. Today's river is considerably less "wild" due to the locks and dams that make it navigable for large river vessels. However, as we use the river, we still can get a little taste of what our forbearers experienced. The next time you cross the Veterans Bridge, or visit the various marinas in our region, take a moment to reflect on just how important our river is.

Skulls of Steubenville

For thousands of years, people have lived right here on this land, and the river and hills serve as an ever-present backdrop that is just as familiar to us today as it was to our ancient ancestors. On this ancient landscape, we can, if we know where to look, find evidence of its earliest inhabitants. I have often imagined finding something here of our distant past; perhaps I might come across an ancient site or maybe a stray arrowhead. I'm still searching.

I love looking at old maps, and one I particularly enjoy is the "Beers-Panhandle" map made in 1871 of the northern counties of West Virginia. Looking closely at the area directly across the river from Steubenville, just south of the ferry where the Market Street Bridge would be built in 1905, one can see there were a few natural features. There was an area consisting of a natural outcropping of rock known as Town Rock. This was a place where the early inhabitants of the area would visit and picnic among the cliffs. You can still find some old postcards that show Town Rock, and evidently it looked similar to the rock shelter in Avella. Just south of this area was Castle Rock, and below that was an "Indian Cave where human skeletons were found." This would be just over the hill from where the people of the Panhandle Archaic Culture had their camp four thousand

Postcard view of Town Rock, located on the West Virginia side of the river opposite Steubenville. *Author's collection.*

years previously. As a historian, I always ask the obvious: What happened to these remains and where did they end up? The answer, I thought, was lost to history. It turns out that the answer was still out there after all, waiting to be rediscovered.

Beginning in 1830, a prominent Philadelphia physician, Dr. Samuel Morton, began collecting cranial specimens, or skulls, from all over the world. His aim was to collect skulls from different ethnic groups and then study and argue the differences between them, among other things. Dr. Morton sent out letters to friends and acquaintances all over the world asking for examples of skulls to be sent for his collection. At some point around the mid-1820s, Dr. Morton met Benjamin Tappan, an attorney, judge, United States senator from Ohio and Steubenville resident. Although it is not clear how Tappan and Morton met, it could have been due to the fact that Tappan's mother was a grandniece of Ben Franklin, giving him a Philadelphia connection. Tappan corresponded with Morton, and when Morton asked for specimens for his cranium collection, Tappan knew just where to look.

In May 1835, a cave was discovered across from Steubenville containing what appeared to be Native American remains. Benjamin Tappan wrote, "The bones appear to have been deposited at different periods of time, those on top being alone in good preservation. They were of all ages and thrown indiscriminately after the removal of the flesh; for it is well known that some tribes were accustomed to gather, at times, all the bones of their deceased relatives, and place them in a common receptacle." Tappan and other prominent folks from Steubenville sent eight skulls found there to Philadelphia, leaving behind many others that were in poor shape. Dr. Morton published his research, including an image of one of the Steubenville skulls, in his 1839 book *Crania Americana*. After Morton died in 1851, his collection of 867 skulls from around the world was donated to the Academy of Natural Sciences in Philadelphia. Later, in the 1960s, it was donated to the University of Pennsylvania Museum of Archaeology and Anthropology, where the collection is housed today.

The cave, Town Rocks and Castle Rock are probably gone, undoubtedly destroyed at some point during the construction of Route 2. The skulls of Steubenville still exist, however, and are an interesting connection between our local history and the wider world.

THE "WILD" LIFE

In most of my professional museum roles over the years, my duties have encompassed a lot. The typical duties one might find in a museum director's job description, such as leading tours, managing the financials and promoting the site, are always to be expected. The part I always noticed, though—and typically, it was at the very bottom of the description, in small print—was "other duties as assigned." This means just that—anything and everything else that may come up. As a former museum director, over the years, I have done many "other duties."

Each job comes with its own particular set of unique issues, but one "other duty" that seems to be present at each of my positions is to encounter wildlife—usually making itself a nuisance. At Historic Fort Steuben, we were constantly battling groundhogs, raccoons and opossums that somehow made it into the place, digging holes and causing their particular sort of mischief. I often think that if it was 1786 and the soldiers and surveyors were still in residence at the fort, many of these creatures would end up invited to dinner—especially in the winter of 1786–87, when supplies from Fort Pitt were disrupted and hunters were employed to bring food in to feed the hungry men. We have no records of the soldiers hunting these particular species, but I think if pressed, they would have indulged. Groundhog, although not my first choice of wild game, can be edible if cooked properly. Don't ask how I know.

With these creatures in mind, the types of wild animals here at the time of the fort and earlier were ones we expect to see, and do still see, now. Moving forward in history, the wildlife of this area and what was considered the backcountry actually was a large reason for the breakout of the French and Indian War of the 1750s. This area could be hunted and contribute to the great wealth of the fur trade in the backcountry. The most valuable skin of all the animals was that of the beaver. Beavers were regarded as living gold due to the fact that their skins were already naturally waterproof and did not need to be treated to make them so. Overhunting critically reduced the population of these creatures in our area, but today, beavers are making a comeback and can be found locally in our streams and river, as can the playful otter that has reportedly been seen in Tomlinson Run State Park.

When Steubenville was established in 1797, wild game was still abundant in our area. One could still make a living as a trapper in the Northwest Territory. As settlements were established specifically in Jefferson County, large predatory game was classified as a nuisance. Officials wanted to reduce these animals in the county, so in 1803, according to the 1897 centennial souvenir publication, "A premium was paid out of the county treasury for the scalp of each wolf or panther killed within the county. For those under six months old the bounty was fifty cents, for those over that age one dollar. This premium was increased on June 3, 1807, to $1.50 and $3.00." There were scores of premiums paid for the scalps of these animals in the early years.

View in Steubenville.

The engraving shows the appearance of Market-street, looking westward, near the Court House, which appears on the right; a portion of the Market on the left; the Steubenville and Indiana Railroad crosses Market-street in the distance, near which are Woolen Factories.

Early nineteenth-century engraving of Steubenville showing Market and Third Streets. The Market House (*left*) and courthouse (*right*) are opposite each other. *Author's collection.*

Over the years, the wolves and panthers of this area were hunted to the brink of extinction, as were the bears. According to Louis Truax in his memoir of life in Weirton, the last recorded bear in the area was killed in 1885 by one Mr. Hindman near South Thirteenth Street on Weirton Heights. The bear had apparently killed some of Mr. Hindman's sheep and lived in the valley known as Bear Run, adjacent to present-day Greenbrier Road. Recently, there was a reported bear cub sighting in Weirton, which would be a first for our area in many years. Maybe bears are returning to their natural habitat after so many years of being absent.

All in all, the wildlife of our area is very rich and diverse. The value of these important species to the culture and history of our area is profound and can even be cited as a major reason for the escalation of historical worldwide conflicts. I suppose it is a good thing these animals are returning to the area. They restore an important natural balance to our native wildlife, and as long as interacting with them is not on my list of "other duties as assigned," we can both live in harmony.

Chapter 2

SETTLEMENT AND DISCOVERY

*A*s a historian, I always look to our landscape to tell a story. I am fascinated by old maps, city plans and blueprints. I am fortunate that in my mind's eye, I have a gift to be able to imagine and almost see a landscape that is gone. All one has to do is study the map. And believe me—I have lost many hours looking at old maps. It is true that our landscape has changed dramatically, not only in the past few decades but in the last two centuries. The two things that have remained constant in those changes, however, are the hills we inhabit and the Ohio River.

In the previous chapter, I mention the river many times, but I can't overestimate the importance of this mighty tributary. The river is quite literally history in and of itself. It has served as a food and water source for at least nineteen thousand years of continuous human habitation in our region. Battles were fought over it, famous individuals descended it and it provided the transportation to get our manufactured products out into the world. It still gives up its water for our coffee and tea and provides recreation and a beautiful backdrop for many stunning pictures of our river cities. Of all that history, one event that took place partly on our local river stands out as one of the most important and historically significant aspects of our national story.

The Lewis and Clark expedition, or the Corps of Discovery, began in 1803 at the direction of President Thomas Jefferson. He had just negotiated with France the purchase of 827,000 acres of land west of the Mississippi River, known as the Louisiana Purchase, for $15 million. The announcement of

Postcard view of the Market Street Bridge looking toward West Virginia. The bridge opened to traffic in 1905. *Author's collection.*

the sale occurred on July 4, 1803, but secretly, Jefferson had been planning an expedition into the West since January, when he sent a secret letter to Congress asking it to authorize funds for an expedition to explore the west to the Pacific Ocean. Meriwether Lewis was chosen specifically by Jefferson to take up this journey. Lewis was Jefferson's former secretary and also a fellow native of Albemarle County, Virginia. On July 5, according to the Thomas Jefferson's Monticello website, Lewis left Washington to begin his journey.

In July, Lewis stopped at Harpers Ferry, Virginia, now West Virginia, for supplies, and eventually, later that month, he arrived in Pittsburgh. While in Pittsburgh, he would oversee the construction of the keelboats he would use in his descent of the river. On August 31, Lewis and eleven men left Pittsburgh on their travel west.

On September 4, 1803, Lewis and his crew passed the boundary of Pennsylvania and Virginia. Ohio, admitted to the Union as its seventeenth state that past March, was on the western shore of the river. The following evening, Lewis and his crew camped on Browns Island and endured a very stormy and wet night. After Lewis's crew set up camp, two of his canoes were still unaccounted for. According to his journal, "Ordered the trumpet to be sounded and they came up in a few minutes." The trumpet was a tool Lewis used to keep in contact with his crew if they were separated by

Steub...ville City Market, Steubenville, Ohio.

Postcard view of the Steubenville City Market building on South Third Street. Today, this building houses municipal offices. *Author's collection.*

signaling with a short, one-note blast. This was used for the first time on Browns Island during the expedition.

Early the next morning, Lewis and his crew set out down the river but were caught up on some riffles, or rocks, in the river about two and a half miles south of the island. Lewis wrote, "Struck on a riffle which we got over with some difficulty and in the distance of two miles and a half passed 4 others, three of which we were obliged to drag over with horses; the man charged me the exorbitant price of two dollars for his trouble." Lewis continued on his way and sailed past Steubenville. In his journal, he described the town. "Stewbenville a small town situated on the Ohio in the state of Ohio about six miles above Charlestown (Wellsburg) in Virginia and 24 above Wheeling—is small well built thriving place has several respectable families residing in it, five years since it was a wilderness." After passing Steubenville, Lewis encountered more trouble: "Got on pretty well to Steuwbenville, which we past at 2 Oc….Struck on a riffle about two miles below the town, hoisted our mainsail to assist in driving us over the riffle, the wind blew so heard as to break the spreat of it, and now having no assistance but by manual exertion and my men, woarn down by perpetual lifting, I was obliged again to have recourse to my usual resort and sent out in serch of horses or oxen." It is clear that this stretch of river was difficult for Lewis and his men to traverse.

The next morning, Lewis and his company passed Charlestown, later Wellsburg, West Virginia, described as "a handsome little village containing about forty houses." Wellsburg later became the home of one of the most well-known participants in the Lewis and Clark expedition, Patrick Gass. Gass joined the group in 1804 after the death of one of the company and became highly regarded. He kept a journal of the expedition that was later published, years before Lewis's own account of the expedition made it to print. The journal eventually was published overseas in French and German and was added to Zadok Cramer's book *The Navigator*, which guided thousands of immigrants to the West. Gass has an interesting history. He was born in 1771 in Falling Springs, Pennsylvania, and eventually moved to "Catfish Camp," later Washington, Pennsylvania, in the 1790s. While in the army, he was stationed at Kaskaskia, Illinois, and it was there that he was recruited for the expedition.

After the Lewis and Clark expedition was completed in 1806, Gass remained in the army. He was a veteran of the War of 1812, in which he lost an eye, and he later moved to Wellsburg, where his father was then living.

Steubenville railroad bridge looking toward West Virginia in July 1888. *Jefferson County Historical Association.*

In 1831, Gass married Maria, the daughter of his friend John Hamilton. She was twenty, and he was fifty-eight, but despite the age difference, they made a happy home. From that union, they had seven children. Maria passed away in 1849, leaving Patrick to care for his large family alone. Not a wealthy man, Gass received $96 a year as a pension for his service in the War of 1812, despite lobbying for better benefits for veterans. In 1867, Patrick was baptized in the Ohio River at Wellsburg and became a member of the Christian church. Finally, in 1870, he passed away at the age of ninety-nine, the last survivor of the famed Lewis and Clark expedition. He is buried in Brooke Cemetery in Wellsburg.

With the passing of Gass, the Lewis and Clark expedition became a thing of history. However, nationally and locally, our connection with this transcendent event in American history is strong. The Ohio River and our area played an important part in the journey. In 2019, Congress expanded the Lewis and Clark Historic Trail to encompass the Ohio River and the route Lewis traveled before he met Clark in 1804. And it is all thanks to the mighty but beautiful Ohio River.

Fort Steuben

Visitors who stop at Historic Fort Steuben are usually surprised to learn not only the history of the fort but also about the history of the site after the fort was abandoned in the late spring of 1787. Construction of the fort began in the fall of 1786 and was completed around February 1787 by the First American Regiment and a group of surveyors assigned to survey the first seven ranges of the Northwest Territory. This land west of the Ohio River had been transferred from England following the Treaty of Paris in 1783, which ended the American Revolution. The cash-strapped government, in an effort to raise funds for the United States' coffers, elected to survey and offer for sale the land of Ohio, and it all began in our area. The government sent out the First American Regiment to protect the surveyors from hostile Native Americans and to remove the "squatters" who had illegally set up homesteads in the new territory. Fort Steuben was built as a winter encampment that was only occupied for eight months, and then the army and surveyors moved on down the river. Fort Steuben's doors were closed in May 1787, but its history didn't end there.

The fort appears again on a map from 1788, and a few travelers moving down the river mention the ruins of Fort Steuben in their writings, but by

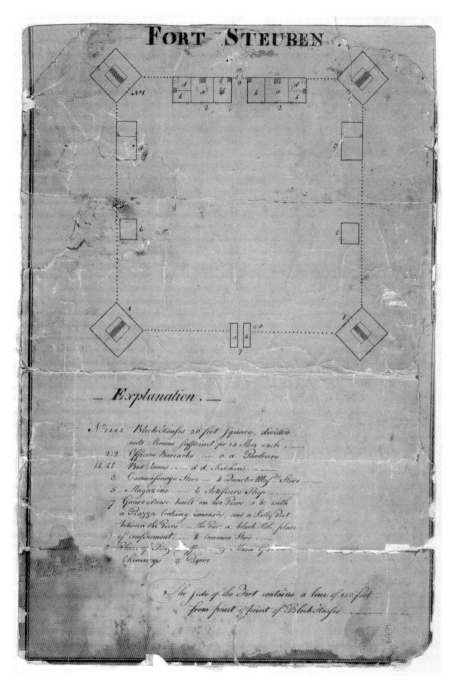

Major Erkuries Beatty's 1787 sketch of Fort Steuben. *Historic Fort Steuben.*

View of the Daugherty block located at Third and Market Streets in 1885. *Jefferson County Historical Association.*

1790, the fort was gone. Oral history, passed down through the years, suggests that the fort was destroyed by fire around 1790. Although archaeological excavations at the site by Franciscan University have been ongoing since 1978, there has been no conclusive evidence that the fort burned down. Our opinion at the visitor center is that after the fort was abandoned, it was possibly parted out as a quarry for timber, finished wood or stone used for the numerous chimneys in the area or lived in by settlers returning to the Ohio Country. In 1890, the people of Steubenville held a commemoration of the burning of Fort Steuben, but there is no evidence that suggests the burning of the fort is accurate. I would like to think that there are some unknown buildings in Steubenville that may have logs from the original fort, but that could be wishful thinking.

Fort Steuben was mentioned again in 1796 in a Pittsburgh newspaper advertising the sale of lots of the town of Steubenville, laid out by James Ross and Bezaleel Wells. The advertisement said lots would be sold from Charlestown, now Wellsburg, West Virginia, and from Fort Steuben. Whether this was the Fort Steuben we know, or the general area around Steubenville, is unclear. What is clear, though, is that the historical location of Fort Steuben was passed on through the oral tradition, considering that the fort would have been long gone by 1796. The block, bounded by Third, Adams, Market and High Streets (now Route 7), has always been associated with the site of the fort. From the 1790s through the late twentieth century, the block was developed into residential lots on High and the south end of Third Street and commercial enterprises on the upper end of Third and Market. What is interesting to me is that in the nineteenth century, folks were looking for remains of the fort. From the discovery of a broadaxe, one of those common to pioneers of the late eighteenth century, to the discovery of a well supposedly used by the soldiers at Fort Steuben, interest never really waned in the story of the fort in our area.

Over the years, many groups tried to rebuild the fort but were not successful. It wasn't until Elizabeth King and her friend Geraldine Cohen attended a lecture given by Dr. Jack Boyd to their group, the American Association of University Women, about his work on the archaeology of historic Fort Steuben, that they were inspired to embark on the reconstruction of the fort in 1986. The rest is history.

It took the Old Fort Steuben Project over 20 years to rebuild historic Fort Steuben, whereas it took the original soldiers only a few months to finish the first Fort Steuben. I think if you could ask the soldiers who occupied the fort in 1787 if they could imagine that over 230 years later, we would be honoring what they did at Fort Steuben, they would be surprised. We are honored to take up the reins of history and hold the fort for future generations to come.

Archaeology at the Fort

One of my wife's numerous wonderful qualities I have discovered over many years of marriage is that she always seems to know just what to say to me or our children when confronted with different situations. Whether it be words of encouragement, advice or the occasional instance when we need to be pushed back on the right track, she is always there to offer a bit of wisdom. I envy her ability to pull out sayings that are appropriate, and one that I constantly need to be reminded of, especially in my profession, is that "the past is another country." That is to say, it is hard for us, in our present frame of mind, to put ourselves back in a distant past, because of our dependence on technology, our culture and the modern worldview, to just name a few reasons. I almost think that it would be an easier transition for someone from the past to come to the present than the other way around.

As historians, we try every day to bring the past to life and do our best to understand the people, places and things that impacted their world. One of the fascinating and effective ways we have done that at Historic Fort Steuben is through archaeology. Since 1978, Franciscan University has led those efforts, first under the direction of Professor Jack Boyde and now under Professor Phillip Fitzgibbons. The finds from these extensive digs over the last forty years have been numerous and include lots of objects that tell the story not just of the fort but also of our early local community stretching until the 1960s, when the block that would have been part of the fort complex was actually turned into a parking lot. A good majority of that lot is still there under about eighty inches of topsoil, forever frustrating anyone who wants to stick something in the ground. The benefit of this lot is that the parking area effectively sealed off the fort's pre-1960s archaeology, preserving it for future discovery.

Right now, the team from Franciscan University is digging an edge of a foundation of a substantial brick home. To identify the place and who lived there is possible, if one knows where to look. There are several maps one can reference that will show the lots laid out presumably in the 1790s by Bezaleel Wells. Our lots in question, which make up the fort area today, are lots 51, 52, 53 and 54. The lots are, generally speaking, 60 feet wide and 161 feet deep with frontage on the now-missing South High Street, essentially Route 7. With the aid of maps and the dimensions of the lots, the team from the university measured out the ground and determined that the building in question was on lot 52. There is a building matching the same size on the earliest known map showing structures in downtown Steubenville in 1856. With the help of the Sanborn fire insurance maps of downtown Steubenville, available on the Library of Congress website, we can discover that the address of the home was 131 South High Street and the owner of the property was Judge John Huston Miller.

Fort Steuben, Steubenville, Ohio.

Postcard view of Historic Fort Steuben. *Author's collection.*

Judge Miller was born on a farm in Northampton County, Pennsylvania, in 1813. He came to Steubenville in 1837 and engaged in the wagon trade, but that life was not for him. Since he was bright and had been gifted a good education, he aspired to be an attorney and studied law under General Samuel Stokely, a local attorney who was later elected to the 1841 U.S. Congress. Miller was admitted to the bar in 1840. In 1841, Judge Miller married Ann Stokely, Samuel's younger sister and daughter of Revolutionary War captain Thomas Stokley. The Millers had two children. According to his 1891 obituary, Judge Miller practiced law in Steubenville for over thirty years and was appointed by future president Rutherford B. Hayes to fill a vacancy as judge of the Common Pleas Court for the Third Subdivision of the Eighth Judicial District. The building located at 131 South High Street actually dates to before 1856 and was owned, at least in the 1870s and '80s, by the Miller family. According to the 1880 census, living at the address was John and his wife; their son, George; their daughter, Elizabeth, with her husband, Henry; and a granddaughter, Maria. Also at the residence was a domestic servant, Mary Canfield, and her daughter Emmeline. In 1882, Ann Miller, John's wife, died and was interred at Union Cemetery. Devout Presbyterians, the Millers were members of First Presbyterian Church, and Ann's funeral was most likely held there, as was John's when he died nine years later. At the time of his death, all of his six siblings were still living except one half brother, Amos, who died while fighting in the Civil War in 1863.

With the excavation of what we believe to be the Miller home, we should eventually run into another property and dwellings located on lot 53. The homes located on that lot, 127 and 125 South High Street, were owned by the Basler family at the same time that the Millers were living in their home in the latter half of the nineteenth century. Joseph and Max Basler, along with their father, Joseph Basler Sr., occupied several dwellings on the east and west side of South High Street. The Baslers were immigrants to the United States from their native Baden, Germany, and upon arriving in Steubenville, they engaged in a variety of businesses, notably a brewery. Basler's Beer Brewery was established in 1836, but by 1852, a new brewery building had been erected directly across South High Street from the Baslers' and Judge Miller's place with the number 130. The business did a good trade in Steubenville for a number of years. In 1875, though, disaster struck when a two-ton boiler exploded on the upper level of the brewery, practically destroying the building and several neighboring residences. The explosion ejected the iron boiler over three hundred feet away. Luckily, no one was seriously injured in the blast. The buildings were rebuilt, and work resumed until 1882, when a fire partially destroyed the facility. That, unfortunately, spelled the end of the Basler brewery.

Today, there is nothing left of South High Street except an overgrown sidewalk near Route 7 that cuts directly through the former site of the Basler Beer Brewery. Looking at the forgotten foundations at the dig in the fort, one can begin to connect the pieces of a forgotten time and bring together the stories of those who have gone before on this same ground. My wife is right that the past is a different country, and we can get there by digging the past. It's our passport to history.

THE ELLIS ISLAND OF THE WEST

Our valley was founded by immigrants. What we know today and what we have here in our valley are the direct results of someone's hard work. These groups of people came here and built a life from nothing into something worth being proud of. The reason people have come to this valley is the thought and the promise of a better life. As a grandson of first-generation Italian and Polish immigrants, whose parents and siblings came to this country with nothing, I am proud that the sacrifices they made to pull themselves out of poverty enabled me to live where I do and have the education I have and gave me the ability to pass their hard work on to my children.

Generally speaking, most of our immigrant ancestors came through Ellis Island in New York City, and Ellis Island has a wonderful website anyone can use to track a family member who came through there, but we are also blessed to have our own little "Ellis Island" right here in Steubenville. Our first Federal Land Office served as the debarkation point for the immigrants and pioneers who settled our region. The fort has visitors all the time who are interested in tracking down a specific relative who may have passed through the land office on their way to points west. Although there is a copy of the names and origins of people who purchased land at the land office from the time the office opened around 1800 to 1812, the fort's staff can also point visitors to the Bureau of Land Management's land office records, which has all that information digitized from 1800 to 1840, when the Steubenville land office closed. Visitors are always amazed when they visit the little building and imagine that their ancestor may have occupied the same space at some point two hundred years earlier.

First Federal Land Office on Sunset Boulevard. The cupola on the roof was used during World War II to watch for enemy planes. It also was the headquarters for the Civil Defense in Jefferson County. *Jefferson County Historical Association.*

A similar situation happened to my wife, Abigail, recently. Although she has mostly Italian ancestry, she also has ancestors that have been in this country for a very long time, going back to at least the seventeenth century. Looking back at her line, we were excited to discover that her fifth, sixth, and seventh great-grandfathers were residents and early pioneers of this area. Abel Johnson, a Revolutionary War veteran, and his wife, Anne, were pioneers and residents of the Ohio Valley around the Colliers, West Virginia, and Eldersville, Pennsylvania area from the late eighteenth century. Abel and Anne had several children and were early members of St. John's Episcopal Church, appearing in the register of parishioners in 1800. St. John's Church on Eldersville Road was founded in 1793 by Pennsylvania-born missionary Dr. Joseph Doddridge and was the first Episcopal church west of the mountains. Today, it is the oldest continually active Episcopal congregation in West Virginia. In 1812, Abel and his son Isaac purchased the northwest quarter of section 34, township 12, range 6, in Harrison County, Ohio. The land patent was issued by David Hoge, the Steubenville

Final move for the first Federal Land Office to its present location on South Third Street, 1976. *Historic Fort Steuben.*

land office registrar. Abel and Anne remained in Brooke County while their son Isaac settled in Harrison County. Abel passed away in 1820, and Anne lived on until she was over one hundred years old, passing in 1850. Both are buried at St. John's Church. The present building was built in 1849, and I would like to think that Anne played a small part in its construction. It is neat to think that my wife, a descendant of these tough frontier folk, can visit the church her ancestors helped found and visit the land office where her folks purchased land to build something out of endless wilderness. As she is the strongest, most giving and caring person I know, I think she inherited part of their spirit.

That is what all our immigrant ancestors did, after all. They came to a land foreign to them, struggled, pulled themselves up and built a life from scratch, and for that, we should be eternally grateful.

Chapter 3

STEUBENVILLE AND JEFFERSON COUNTY

I love old houses and the stories they can tell us of the past. I have always wanted to live in an old home and learn its history, but as of yet, I have not fulfilled that dream. My house growing up was built by my parents in the 1980s, and my grandparents' homes were built by them in the 1950s. Those homes have a history now, too, to be sure, but it is not the same as that of a Queen Anne–style home, or a Colonial, Federal, Gothic or Italianate structure. Truly, though, most of us aren't lucky enough to inhabit a high-style example of a previous trend in architecture. After watching a lot of HGTV, I am not sure many would want to, either. Most of us live in vernacular examples that are reminiscent of those styles, and that's great, too.

My wife and I take pride in identifying vernacular architecture, and it has become a kind of game for us. As we travel, we often point out old houses and buildings and see who is first to identify the right style. And if we disagree, we can defend our various platforms. Driving slowly and looking around at buildings does possibly pose a hazard to other drivers, so we have thought of getting a bumper sticker that reads "Will Brake for Architecture." Let's just say that I am extremely fortunate to have a wife and a life companion who shares a quirky and similar interest in history.

It is true to say that we have lost more than a few unique buildings in our area. There are even fewer left that can be identified as striking examples of specific types of architecture. And when you find one still standing, it is exciting. Looking at downtown Steubenville, many of the early nineteenth-

Postcard view of the Grove, built by Bezaleel Wells in 1798. *Author's collection.*

century stately homes have long since vanished. One that I come across often in my research that played an important part in our town's early history was built by our town's founder, Bezaleel Wells, and was dubbed the Grove.

The Grove was a stately Federal-style house built of brick on a large plot of land in the southern end of Steubenville. Today, the site is located south of the intersection of Slack and South High Streets, very near the abandoned Weirton Steel Office, and is just east of the intersection of South Third Street and Route 7. When Bezaleel began construction of his home in 1798, he had already finished laying out the city lots and streets that would become the city of Steubenville. For his own holdings, he settled on 412 acres just south of his settlement. The building was made up of three parts. Although there aren't any existing floor plans or prints that I am aware of, using primary source evidence and existing pictures of the mansion, we can get a good idea of its layout. In any case, what follows is my best educated guess. The central core of the house was two and a half stories and most likely comprised the main formal and entertaining spaces of the house. There was a central hall with a unique sweeping, curving iron grand stairway that led to the upper floor bedchambers. The stairs were in a circular hall in the rear of the building at the end of the central hall. Some houses of this period would have a special bedchamber on the first floor that was saved for important guests or important events in the life of the family, like births, wedding nights

Postcard view of the interior of the Grove. *Author's collection.*

and, unfortunately, deaths. I am not certain the Grove had any such room, at least in this section of the house.

The two other wings of the great house, to the left and right of the main section, were two-story brick buildings connected to the main section by short, one-story passages. Each of the passages had an exterior door and a window for ventilation in the days before AC. The left wing of the house most likely housed the dining room, because after investigating existing Sanborn fire insurance maps, I have determined that there is an outbuilding located directly behind this section that is separate from the main structure. This is almost sure to have been a summer kitchen. The summer kitchen would have been a separate structure due to the fact that in the summer, one would not want the kitchen near the living space, adding the heat of the cooking fire to their lodging. Also, the risk of fire was decreased if the buildings were separate. Just like today, in that period, the kitchen was usually located near the dining room, so it would make sense that this wing housed that room. A winter kitchen could have been located under this wing, in a basement, but that is speculation. Also in the wing could have been another sitting room and on the upper floors, rooms for live-in help. My guess would be that the right wing housed the less formal, everyday living spaces of the house, perhaps a few bedrooms, a nursery, a living room or a second dining room where less formal meals were taken. All in all, the house was a mansion, considering many houses in the area at this time were log or wooden frame structures at best.

Bezaleel moved into his home in 1800 and stayed in residence there for the next thirty or so years. He had been widowed in 1797 and had also lost two daughters prior to his wife's passing, but he remarried in 1798 to Sarah Griffith Wells, and they had six sons and five daughters. The Grove had plenty of room for this large family. It was the social center of town, and it has been reported in a number of publications that many prominent visitors were guests, like Henry Clay and, in 1821, Chief Justice Salmon Chase, who "stopped at the hospitable mansion of Mr. Wells…his beautiful place on the banks of the Ohio…and with his pleasant family, passed some very agreeable days."

Hard times, unfortunately, fell on the Wells family, and the Grove was ultimately sold around 1830 to General Samuel Stokely. Here, the Stokely family and their descendants passed the next sixty years. The house was then known as Stokely's Grove and was still the center of social gatherings in our city. Stokely was the land receiver at the Steubenville Land Office in 1827, state senator in 1837 and, finally, a U.S. congressman from 1841 to 1843. In 1861, Stokely died and passed the home to his daughter Jane and her husband, Colonel William R. Lloyd. Colonel Lloyd fought in the Civil War with the Sixth Ohio Cavalry, of which he was the commanding officer until he resigned shortly before the regiment saw action at Gettysburg in 1863. I can only imagine the conversations that took place at the Grove during that time.

In 1877, Lloyd passed away and left the home to his wife and remaining children. By 1902, the property had been sold, and the site was to be redeveloped into the Pope Tin Mill Plant and, later, Weirton Steel's Steubenville plant. According to a *Herald Star* article in March 1902, "Workmen commenced demolishing the old Bezaleel Well residence.… The big steam shovels cut away the hills close up on each side of the historic old manor house and now it must go.…Even the hill upon which it stood was to disappear." While demolishing the home, according to another article in April 1902, relics of the past were found in the ruin, such as a land grant signed in 1785 by Virginia governor Patrick Henry, legal land documents from the eighteenth century and a letter written by President William Henry Harrison in 1836. Many books and newspapers were found going back to the 1820s and '30s, as well. By June 1902, the whole site had been transformed into an industrial site, and to this day, it bears no resemblance to its former history.

The Grove passed from our landscape in 1902, but the history of the impressive place still resonates in our town's story. In Joseph Doyle's book *History of Jefferson County*, he recounts a poem about the old place that appeared in the *Herald* on April 8, 1820:

Near where Ohio's flowing waters glide,
And Nature counts the sun's resplendent rays,
The enchanting Castle, well of man the pride,
Arrests the passing stranger's wistful gaze.
Here fancy and simplicity unite,
And taste and culture happily combine,
Delightful spot, where fruits and flowers invite,
Where clusters tempt, and fruitful vines entwine.

Even though the old house is gone, we can still hear its story.

REACHING STANTON

As a public historian, my goal, in a nutshell, is connecting the present with the past. And one of the first steps in making that connection is to find common ground between the ages. For me personally, there is something compelling about walking the same streets, visiting the same places and talking about the same things as those who went before us. In this way, the past does not seem so distant.

One figure who is difficult to connect with in local history is Steubenville native Edwin Stanton. He is one of those figures who looms larger than life. As President Abraham Lincoln's secretary of war during the Civil War, Stanton's influence in national events is far-reaching, to put it mildly. Many books and articles have been written about him, his influences and his accomplishments. And it was Stanton who famously uttered the words after President Lincoln's assassination: "Now he belongs to the ages."

Reconstructing the Steubenville that Edwin Stanton knew is a tall order. Considering that Stanton was born in 1814 and spent the better half of his young adulthood in Steubenville before moving to Pittsburgh in 1847, a lot is now different. If Stanton were to return today and walk the streets of his hometown, he would find the courthouse changed, the city building gone and his boyhood home and birthplace demolished. However, strolling up Market Street, he would come face to face with a home he knew personally.

View of North Fourth Street, circa 1869. *Jefferson County Historical Association.*

Today, that building is located at 644 Market Street and was most recently the Urban Thrift and Opportunity Center, part of the Urban Mission, but years ago, it was the City Rescue Mission. A lot has changed since Stanton last saw the building. Most notably, the large front porch, the turret in the Queen Anne style and additions to the back of the building would be new to him, as they were added at some point after 1897.

Built circa 1824, the core of the building is one of the oldest structures known to exist in downtown Steubenville. It was built by Connecticut native Daniel Lewis Collier, who was born in 1796. Collier immigrated to Steubenville around 1816, supposedly floating on a raft down the Ohio River. His brother James followed soon after, in 1820. Both Collier brothers became successful lawyers. James went on to run for Ohio governor for the Whig Party but lost.

Daniel, although not as politically active as his brother, remained in Steubenville, working at his successful law practice. The Stanton family was well acquainted with Collier. In 1827, when Edwin Stanton was just

Photograph of Edwin Stanton. *Historic Fort Steuben.*

thirteen years old, his father died, leaving his mother widowed with four children to raise. Daniel Collier became Stanton's guardian and the executor of his father's estate. Stanton relied on Collier for advice and, in all practical matters, considered Collier a father figure. Letters surviving after all these years between Stanton and Collier are formal but also familiar. In the book *Stanton* by Walter Stahr, it is recorded that it was young Edwin who asked Collier if it was possible to have a loan from the estate for him to attend Kenyon College in 1831. His stay at Kenyon was short-lived, for in August 1832, he wrote Collier and asked if there was more money for him to continue his studies, to which Collier replied that he needed to work for funds instead of spending on education. According to Stahr, it took Collier some time to convince Stanton that returning to college and retaining debt was a bad idea. So, Stanton worked for another Steubenville businessman, James Turnbull, in Columbus. Fast-forward a few years after Stanton was admitted to the bar in Jefferson County in December 1835, and it was Collier who allowed Stanton to argue some cases on his behalf. Stahr recounts in his book that a question was raised about Stanton's qualifications to argue a case in court. Collier, addressing the room, said, "Although Stanton was not quite twenty-one he was 'as well qualified to practice law as Collier himself or any other attorney of this bar'…and Stanton pitched right in again without waiting for the Judge to rule on the motion."

After a successful career in Steubenville, Stanton moved on to bigger and brighter things, but he was still in touch with Collier for the rest of their lives. Both of them died within months of each other in 1869. Stanton was nominated by President Grant and confirmed by the Senate to be a justice of the Supreme Court on December 20, but he died four days later on Christmas Eve 1869. Collier remained in Steubenville until around 1857, when he moved to Philadelphia. It had to have been around that time that Collier sold his Market Street residence, where he had lived for more than thirty years and raised nine children, to Dr. Thomas Johnson.

Johnson came to Steubenville around 1840 and was prominent in the community. He and his family lived in the grand home during the Civil War

The home of Daniel L. Collier on Market Street, photographed on September 20, 1856. Daniel and his wife are standing in the yard (*right*). *Jefferson County Historical Association.*

and remain its longest private residents. One of their children, Catherine, married Robert Sherrard in 1881. Dr. Johnson died in 1879, and his wife remained in the home until her death in 1900.

It is after the Johnson family moved out that the history of the home becomes a bit murky. There were a few inhabitants of the place between 1900 and 1915. A family called Banfield lived there and advertised for a washwoman during their occupancy. Likely around 1909, Mr. and Mrs. E.T. Weir, founder of Weirton Steel and later National Steel, moved in. I would like to believe that early discussions and decisions about the future of the industrial Ohio Valley were made there. Sometime between 1910 and 1915, the W.H. Lowe family were in residence, and it was the Lowes who sold the place to the D.F. Coe Funeral Home in 1915. Ira McClave purchased the business in 1928, and it was renamed the McClave Funeral Home. This business moved from the building in 1939. Sometime after this, the Cole Brothers Funeral Home took over the building and inhabited it for many years until it became the City Rescue Mission and, finally, part of the Urban Mission.

Post–Civil War view of North Fourth Street. The fire station can be seen in the distance. *Jefferson County Historical Association.*

In your mind's eye, it is easy to imagine young Edwin Stanton meeting with Daniel Collier in the cavernous rooms, discussing his bright future. And we can connect with Stanton the youth, not the imposing man standing with Lincoln during the Civil War, and that makes all the difference.

The Grand Opera House

Recently, my wife and I were fortunate to go to Pittsburgh and see the opera *Carmen* put on by Pittsburgh Opera. The performance was spectacular. The music by the live orchestra, coupled with the acting and spot-on sets in the glamourous Benedum Center, was nothing short of amazing. It wasn't the first time we had seen the production. The last time *Carmen* was performed in Pittsburgh was in 2015, and my wife and I saw it then, too. We love going to the opera. In fact, one of our first dates was a trip to the Benedum to see *The Barber of Seville*, Gioachino Rossini's 1816 masterpiece. Even though the majority of operas performed at the Benedum are extremely old, the themes, storylines and passion of the productions still resonate with a modern viewer. Pittsburgh Opera does a fantastic job of making their performances come alive. The opera *Carmen*, for example, was first performed at the Opéra-Comique in Paris on March 3, 1875, according to the program. In this way, we are able to get in touch with our past. Listening to music and seeing a performance that might have been known by past generations is something appealing to an antiquarian and therefore right up my alley.

Today, for folks in the Upper Ohio Valley, the closest place to see a large opera like *Carmen* would be in Pittsburgh, but that was not always the case. Once upon a time, right here in Steubenville, there were at least two opera houses operating in the city. According to Dr. John Holmes in his book *Remembering Steubenville*, Kilgore Hall, built in 1830 on Market Street between Fifth and Sixth Streets, was the premier venue for stage performances in town. By 1868, though, larger-scale shows were touring the country and needed larger spaces for their productions. According to Holmes, in that year, the Grand English Opera Company was touring the United States with prima donna Euphrosyne Parepa-Rosa. Performances were held in Pittsburgh and Wheeling but not Steubenville, because there was no hall suitable for the show. With that in the minds of the city elite, Kilgore Hall was purchased by H.G. Garrett in 1869 and underwent substantial renovations, including a larger stage, trapdoors, eighty gas jets for lighting and seating for one thousand guests.

Garrett's was the only theater in town large enough for grand performances, but all that changed in 1883 when the City of Steubenville entered the theater business. That year, Steubenville built its new city building on the lot previously occupied by the market house. This lot is now the large green space next to the current city building on Market Street across from the courthouse today. This building, according to the 1897 centennial souvenir

View of South Fourth Street from the corner of Market Street. *Jefferson County Historical Association.*

book, cost $65,000 to construct, with Messrs. Fickes and Kell as contractors. The brick building was three stories tall, with the ground floor occupied by the post office, public library, Board of Education, council chamber, offices of the waterworks, city clerk, street commissioners and two storage rooms. The mayor's office, solicitor and Board of Education rooms were on the upper floors. What comprised the majority of the second and third floor was the City Opera House. City solicitor Charles Reynolds operated

Postcard view of the Steubenville city building and the Grand Opera House. *Author's collection.*

the theater for the city. The first performance took place on August 27, 1883, with the production of *The Lights o' London*. The show premiered at the Princess Theater in London in September 1881 and by 1883 was traveling in the New World. Many members of the original cast performed in Steubenville, and the Wheeling Opera-House orchestra provided the music. Over the next several years, many shows were held in the theater, although the city leased out management of the facility after only one year. The theater eventually became known as the Victoria Theater.

Around the time that the City Opera House opened, a well-known city resident and opera singer was making headlines in New York and Boston for his performances. William H. MacDonald was born here in 1849 and at an early age excelled in singing. In 1873, MacDonald, along with three other Steubenville natives interested in making it in the arts, disembarked for Europe to study their craft. MacDonald studied in Germany and England and in Italy for four years, perfecting his vocal talent. When he returned to the States, he joined a group of performers known as the Bostonians and became part owner. This group became one of the first successful national

Left: Signed 1896
photograph of
Steubenville actor
William MacDonald.
Author's collection.

Below: Postcard view
of Union Cemetery
featuring a parklike
setting. *Author's collection.*

In Union Cemetery, Steubenville, O.

touring companies and is credited for making English opera popular in the United States. With MacDonald as co-owner of the company, it produced many wildly popular shows, including *H.M.S. Pinafore* in 1879, *Prince Ananias* in 1894 and *The Serenade* in 1897, among many others. By far the most well-known production was *Robin Hood* in 1890. This production traveled the country and was extremely popular in its day, performing over two thousand times. It made the Bostonians, and William H. MacDonald, who played the role of Little John, a household name. MacDonald married another well-known singer from Boston called Maria Stone, also a member of the troupe. In 1900, the *Steubenville Herald Star* called him the most popular singer in the United States. In 1905, the Bostonians, due to many different reasons, closed their company. MacDonald went on to perform in other productions with his business partner Henry Clay Barnabee. Tragically, in March 1906, while in Springfield, Massachusetts, for a production of *The Free-Lance*, an opera by John Philip Sousa, MacDonald unexpectedly passed away at the age of fifty-six. Although successful, he had made no provision for his widow, and a benefit was held in New York City in December 1906 by the theater elite to help Mrs. MacDonald and Mr. Barnabee financially, ultimately raising over $20,000. William MacDonald's remains were returned to Steubenville, and he was interred in Union Cemetery at his family plot.

MacDonald is known to have performed with his company at least three times at the Opera House in Steubenville, and according to Joseph Doyle in his book *History of Steubenville and Jefferson County*, proceeds from the performances went to the erection of the Stanton Monument. The Opera House in Steubenville survived as a theater until the late 1920s. In 1929, the city building was demolished to make way for what was known as the City Building Annex. Today, that building is gone, too, replaced with the lovely green space that is more in keeping with how it looked when Bezaleel Wells donated the property to the city so long ago. Looking at pictures of the city building and opera house, I can only imagine what it was like to attend a show there. It certainly would have been a destination for my wife and me. But since it is gone, I can only close my eyes and imagine that I am witnessing a great performance and lovely music. And that suits my old soul well.

SHERRARD HISTORY

Historical research is exciting to me. The thrill of the hunt, the discovery of the story and the sharing of it are what I look forward to every time I descend the historical rabbit hole, following a lead to a great story. I fall victim to leads in history all the time. One story leads to another, and I am off on a tangent discovering a little-known fact. Most of the time, this turns into an interesting story.

This story began with a search for Civil War veterans and ended up in a parking lot on North Fourth Street in Steubenville. The parking lot in question is located at 205 North Fourth Street at the northwest corner of North Fourth and Washington Streets. This lot was not always a parking lot; it once was a large mansion owned by a prominent family. According to the *1897 Centennial Souvenir of Steubenville and Jefferson County*, the Sherrard home was built in 1870 by Justin G. Morris. It boasted twelve large rooms and was appointed with walnut accents. In 1884, the home was purchased by Robert Sherrard Jr. and was extensively remodeled.

Robert Sherrard was born in 1823 on Rush Run, but his family moved to a farm on Coal Hill in the 1840s. Robert was admitted to the bar in 1848 and became a successful lawyer. Due to his success in his profession, in 1850, Robert became a partner with Judge John Miller, who, coincidentally, owned a large home on the corner of Adams and High Streets, the site of the excavations of Fort Steuben. Robert served as a senator in 1861 but ultimately declined a second term.

Sherrard wanted to join the Union cause during the Civil War, but due to "heart trouble" was unable to do so. He did get to participate in the excitement surrounding the presence of Morgan's Raiders in 1864. Joseph Doyle, in his tome *Twentieth Century History of Steubenville and Jefferson County*, explains, "Mr. Sherrard was to take charge of two regiments sent from Pittsburgh to intercept Morgan. The executive ability shown by Mr. Sherrard in circumventing Morgan and forcing him to abandon his plan of crossing the Ohio at the mouth of Short Creek, into West Virginia, gave unmistakable evidence of military and tactical skill. Morgan was forced to move to the north end of the county where he was captured." Sherrard was instrumental in this military operation.

Even during the tumultuous period of the Civil War, in 1863, Robert purchased the Mechanics' Savings Bank, effectively changing his career. In 1870, Robert moved to New York City, where he became the president of American National Bank. By 1877, Robert and his family had returned to Steubenville, when he took over the presidency of the Steubenville Coal and Mining Company. In 1879, he also took over the position of the Steubenville Gas Light and Coke Company. He was one of the founders of the Steubenville Pottery in 1881, as well as the Steubenville Street Railway Company.

Looking west on Market Street during a Steubenville city celebration. The city building is at left. *Jefferson County Historical Association.*

As one can imagine, the Sherrard family was obviously wealthy and prominent in the community. Sherrard and his family took trips often to Europe, Egypt and the Holy Land, and his collection of antiquities was impressive. Surely, the halls of his residence were full of these rare objects, and he delighted in showing them off to his many friends and guests to his home.

In April 1891, the Sherrard home played host to former president Rutherford B. Hayes. Hayes traveled to Steubenville on his way to attend the GAR state encampment. Hayes writes, "I was met at the station in Steubenville by Mr. Robert Sherrard and taken to his hospitable and excellent home. The Sherrards at Steubenville made me at home in the most agreeable way three nights and days."

Hayes had visited Steubenville previously while he was governor of Ohio, and his experience then was not a good one. He arrived by train from Columbus around three thirty in the morning in May 1870 and had to wander the streets of Steubenville searching for the United States Hotel, which was located on Market Street. Arriving at the hotel, Hayes could not

awaken the staff for accommodations and ended up walking the streets of Steubenville again until daylight. Hayes eventually fell asleep in the ladies' parlor of the hotel, where a maid found him and finally gave him a small room. Hopefully, Hayes forgave the sleeping staff!

Sherrard entertained his friend and future United States president William McKinley at his residence in Steubenville, as well. And it was during a drive in an open carriage around Steubenville on November 3, 1895, with Ohio governor McKinley that Sherrard took ill. He passed away at his residence on November 8 at the age of seventy-two. His life and death were chronicled in the newspaper along with descriptions of the services at the First Presbyterian

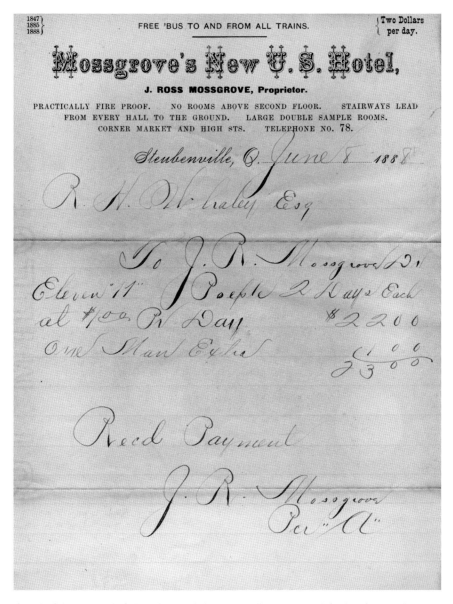

Opposite: Mossgrove's U.S. Hotel, one of the most well-known hotels in the nineteenth century in Steubenville. *Jefferson County Historical Association.*

Above: Mossgrove's U.S. Hotel receipt dated June 8, 1888. This stay was for a visiting baseball team. *Author's collection.*

Church, many telegrams of condolence from famous people and descriptions of the many flower arrangements sent to the family in his memory.

Robert Sherrard was interred at the family mausoleum located in Union Cemetery, of which he was, during his life, a trustee. And if you are familiar with the cemetery, you may know the Sherrard mausoleum as one of the grandest in the place—a fitting resting place for such a prominent member of our community.

The Sherrard home, once a palatial residence that hosted presidents and statesmen, is now barely a memory. It exists only in stories and history books of our illustrious past. And that's the thrill of the hunt; you never know which empty parking lot holds a lot of history.

THOMAS COLE IN STEUBENVILLE

I will never be so boastful as to say that I know the most about the history of our area. How can any one person ever come close to knowing all there is to know about our history? I am constantly reminded, or rather astounded by, all the connections, stories, topics and people that have impacted our area over the years. I am ever aware of what I don't know rather than what I do know about our area.

One of those interesting connections that I did not know about was Steubenville's connection to artist Thomas Cole. I had always associated the celebrated artist with Upstate New York and the Hudson River. He is credited with founding the Hudson River School style of painting, after all. His landscapes are beautiful and have a dreamlike quality to them. I think they are appealing because they show the wildness and vastness of the American landscape in an era when settlers and pioneers were traversing the mountains and moving west. Cole's works are sought-after and valuable. My wife's favorite painting of his, *The Oxbow* (1836), is on view at the Metropolitan Museum of Art.

Cole was born in Bolton-le-Moors, Lancashire, England, in February 1801, but by 1818, the family had immigrated to Philadelphia, where his father, James, set up a dry goods store. By 1819, the family was on the move again, this time to Steubenville, where Cole's ever-intrepid father had engaged in the wallpaper business. In August 1820, James advertised his new establishment in the *Western Herald & Steubenville Gazette*: "James Cole respectfully informs the public, that he has now on hand, of his own manufacture, a quantity of Paper Hangings, of Various Patterns, which can

South side of Fourth and Market showing the varied architecture of the city of Steubenville. *Jefferson County Historical Association.*

be had, on application at the manufactory in Fourth Street, Steubenville." Young Thomas did have a hand in the business, if nothing else in helping his father make wood engravings, as he had done in their Philadelphia shop.

There is another advertisement in the *Western Herald & Steubenville Gazette* from July 1819 that mentions two Cole sisters, the Misses M. and A. Cole, who had opened a "Seminary for Young Ladies." These young ladies Cole could be Thomas's sisters Mary and Ann. The school was not a religious seminary but rather a boarding and day school that, according to the 1819 advertisement, taught reading, writing, arithmetic, English grammar, geography, history, music, drawing and painting, plain sewing and "all kinds of ornamental and fancy work." The school was located in a "large and commodious house" on Third Street, not far from the Coles' home near the corner of Fourth and Market Streets. The family must have been successful in their business endeavors, as an 1933 article in the *Herald Star*, reminiscing about the Coles' time in Steubenville, mentioned that they were the only family in the region to have a piano. The article continues, "The two daughters of the house, Sarah and Annie, played on the instrument and it was deemed so wonderful that each evening a listening crowd would fill the street from curb to curb to hear the sweet strains."

Cole's historians believe it was here in Steubenville that he made the decision to be an artist. It was common in the nineteenth century for itinerant artists to travel to cities and towns advertising their professional services. Often, artists would set up in a boardinghouse and take on clients until they raised enough funds to move on to their next destination. Around 1820, one of these traveling artists, a fellow called Stein, came to Steubenville and serendipitously met Thomas Cole. According to the New York State Library, which houses the Thomas Cole papers, Stein "taught him the rudiments of mixing color and lent him a treatise on the theory of color." Cole's early studies and sketches included our area, especially the Ohio River and Half Moon Farm, to be exact. Before meeting Stein, Thomas had begun to teach painting in his sisters' school. An advertisement for the seminary in the *Western Herald* announces that "Thomas Cole will instruct a class of males and females in painting and drawing."

By 1823, though, the wallpaper business was failing, and the family removed to Pittsburgh, where James started a business making floor coverings. Eventually, the family settled in New York City. Thomas didn't stay with the family long. As a young and successful painter, at first painting portraits, he moved on to bigger and brighter things, traveling abroad in Europe and, most importantly, discovering the Catskills and Upstate New York, launching the Hudson River School style of painting so renowned in art history.

Thomas Cole died in February 1848 in Catskill, New York. It is not known if Cole or any member of his family ever returned to Steubenville or the Ohio Valley, but the impact of the area made a lasting impression on one of the most influential American landscape painters of the nineteenth century.

THE BASEBALL GREAT

I love opening day for baseball with my son down at the Weirton Baseball Association at the fields on Kings Creek. I never played there as a kid but rather out at the Termite Fields in Paris, Pennsylvania. Still, it is great to go down to Kings Creek, and catch up with folks you don't see often, have a hotdog or some popcorn and, most importantly, watch a good game of baseball.

There are great games that are played here in our area, but if you want some professional action, you must go to Pittsburgh or Cleveland to see the major league players. But there was a time in our area's history when one didn't have to travel far to see a league game. Naturally, in our little communities, we didn't have the means of supporting a major league club, but that didn't stop us from producing some memorable minor league teams, though.

The game of baseball in our area goes back some distance into history. During the Civil War, baseball was introduced to soldiers who met with others from different parts of the country, and although the game wasn't invented during the conflict, the Civil War certainly helped make it popular. Right after the war, in Steubenville, one of the first—if not *the* first—baseball clubs in the city was organized, called the Mears Club. According to an article in the *Daily Herald* dated March 20, 1886, the club was organized in 1866 and played "numerous first-class ball organizations in that day." The first game began on May 11, 1867, at 1:15 p.m. and lasted until 5:20 p.m., with the Mears taking on the Hygeia Club of Pittsburgh. The Mears were victorious with a score of 89–61. To me, that seems like a huge score for a baseball game, but according to an article published in *Smithsonian Magazine* called "A Brief History of the Baseball," the balls of that era were not uniform and were almost always handmade. These balls were made with one piece of leather and four lines of stitching, giving them the nickname "lemon peel." They were lighter, darker in color and softer than the baseballs of today, with a rubber core, and according to the article, they could be hit farther and bounce higher, thus the reason for the high score. But that score was nothing compared to the August 1867 game between Steubenville and Benwood, West Virginia, in which Steubenville prevailed 101–28. The Mears Club played until 1869.

By the early 1880s, a semiprofessional baseball team had been formed here, but it played only local teams. In 1887, the Steubenville Stubs were formed as part of the Ohio State League, which played for only one year.

In 1895, the Stubs were reborn to be part of the Interstate League, with teams from Ohio, Indiana, Michigan, Kentucky and West Virginia. By midyear, the Steubenville Stubs moved to Akron, then to Lima and finally disbanded. In 1906, 1907, 1909, 1911, 1912 and 1913, the Stubs played in a variety of leagues, finally permanently disbanding in 1913—but not before a baseball legend played for his first minor-league team, the Steubenville Stubs, in 1895.

Honus Wagner was born in Carnegie, Pennsylvania, in 1874 and was one of nine children. He dropped out of school at the age of twelve to help support his family by working in a coal mine. Later, he trained as a barber. Reflecting on his past baseball career in 1916, Wagner wrote in the *Pittsburgh Post-Gazette* that it was his brother Al "Butts" Wagner who introduced him to the game. Honus wrote, "In my boyhood, Al was rated among the greatest ball players of the Western Pennsylvania District, but, aside from my pride in his reputation, I did not respond very readily to the wiles of baseball. Al, I thought, was the real ball player of the family and one was enough." It was Al who brought his brother Honus to Steubenville, since in 1895, Al was playing for the Stubs during their season in the Interstate League. Honus recounted,

> *This is how I got to Steubenville. My brother was with the team, and he was the real star of the period, while I was only a proud brother, glad of the privilege of sometimes making a trip and doing the trainer's duties or carrying water. I went there as a pitcher in 1895 and in my first game they played me in the outfield. I muffed three flies and hit a home run but the homer did not get back the runs caused by my muffs and I quit the team and went back to old Carnegie on a freight. Al came after me hot-footed and I rejoined the club.*

Honus wasn't the best pitcher for Steubenville. "One day while pitching, I hit seven men, walked twelve, struck out fifteen and demoralized the Akron Club. After I had broken one man's ribs they insisted that I be taken out and threatened a court injunction to prevent a dangerous man like me from pitching." When he was not on the field with Steubenville, Honus acted as the club's barber, and every Sunday morning, he would shave the team, starting with his brother Al.

By 1897, Honus was playing for the Louisville Colonels, a National League team, but he played only a few seasons for them before he went to play for the Pittsburgh Pirates in 1900 due to the National League being

Steubenville Base Ball Club, Champions P. O. M. League.
1 McIlveen. 2 Sinclair (Backer). 3 Roy. 4 Murphy. 5 Miller. 6 McHale. 7 McCabe. 8 Dr. Laughlin (Bus. Mgr.) 9 Tamsett. 10 Desseau. 11 Stettler (Mgr.) 12 Ortlieb. 13 Connor. 14 Boyle. 15 Pleiss. 16 Murray. 17 Lloyd. 18 Godwin.

The Steubenville Baseball Club, with Dohrman Sinclair listed as the "backer" for the team. *Author's collection.*

reduced from twelve teams to eight. The owner of the Colonels, Barney Dreyfuss, became part owner of the Pirates in that year and took Honus to Pittsburgh. For the Pirates, Honus became a star and helped them get to the very first World Series against the Boston Americans, although the Pirates were defeated five games to three.

Honus returned to Steubenville with the Pirates to play an exhibition game against the Steubenville Business College on October 12, 1905, at Altamont Park. The weather was wintry, but according to the *Herald Star*, over five hundred fans came out to enjoy the game. The Pirates defeated Steubenville 5–3, but Honus was evidently impressed with the local team, because he agreed to come back eight days later for a rematch. Steubenville lost that game too, 7–3.

Honus played major league ball until 1917, when he retired from the Pirates. His batting average was .329, and he had 3,430 hits, 101 home runs, 1,732 RBIs and 722 career stolen bases. In 1911, Honus won his eighth National League batting title. The title was matched only once, in 1997, by Tony Gwynn. In 1915, Honus became the oldest player to hit a grand slam, a record that stood for seventy years, broken only in 1985 by Tony Perez. After retirement, Honus went on to play for some semipro teams, especially the Superior Steel of Carnegie, Pennsylvania, which battled Steubenville's LaBelle Iron Works Team in August 1919. For that game, held on Carnegie Field in the North End, according to the *Herald Star*, three thousand fans turned out to see the old star play one last time. He was cheered every time he went to bat. A special rule was lobbied against him from the Steubenville team to the effect that he could take only two bases on any hit. Despite the rule, Steubenville lost 9–0. Later, in 1933, Honus went on to coach for the Pirates until his death in 1955. His number, 33, was retired in 1952.

Honus was inducted into the Baseball Hall of Fame in its inaugural class of 1936 along with Ty Cobb and Babe Ruth. He is regarded as the best shortstop of all time, and one of his baseball cards, in August 2021, sold for a record $6.6 million, making it the highest-selling sports card of all time. It's incredible to think that this legend had his start right here in Steubenville. It could be that the next Honus Wagner is playing down at the WBA Fields on Kings Creek today. Don't forget to get the baseball card.

The Hub

As we all know, this area has changed through the years. As someone who grew up at the very end of a very prosperous time in our valley's history, I was reminded growing up of what once was, what was here and what we have lost. Not all of it, though, is based on local industry, although that plays a part; it's based on national trends, as well. One trend that prevailed nationally in the 1970s to '80s was the death of the smaller mom-and-pop store and the rise of the malls, with new stores and better parking. And that made anchor stores in downtown areas, such as ours in Steubenville, decline.

One of the places folks miss the most is the Hub. I have heard folks from all over the region remember this store, which was so unique. Luckily for me, my colleagues at Historic Fort Steuben fondly remember Steubenville's anchor store and supplied their memories for this section. The Hub, owned by brothers Mone and Simon Anathan, opened in 1904 on the corner of Fifth and Market Streets as an exclusive men's clothing shop. By 1909, it had expanded to another building and began offering women's and children's clothing and housewares. Business boomed, and plans were drawn up for an expansion in 1916. The First World War put new construction projects on hold, and it wasn't until 1922 that the Hub we remember was completed.

Postcard view of Market Street in Steubenville. The famous Hub department store is at left. *Author's collection.*

The new building, featuring five floors of merchandise, was a store unlike others in the region. Top-quality, higher-end merchandise filled the various departments, and they were all connected by a pneumatic tube system for orders and communication between departments. Going shopping in those days was an event. Men wore hats and suits, while women dressed up wearing hats, dresses and gloves. One never went shopping without gloves! The front door to the Hub was located on Market Street, but most shoppers used the door located around the corner on Fifth Street, the one closest to the parking lot. Employees used this door, too, as it was nearest to the time clock.

The Hub was truly a department store in every modern sense. The first floor featured men's shoes and casual wear, sporting goods and ladies' sporting wear, candy, cosmetics, intimates, jewelry, linens, cards and giftwrap, books and records, run by National Record Mart, as well as the credit department. Notions were also on the first floor, where you could purchase thread, ribbon and the like. The second floor hosted ladies' dresses and coats, bridal and ladies' shoes, hats and intimates, in addition to junior girls' clothing and Girl Scout and school uniforms. The third floor featured toys, appliances, housewares and china, men's suits (with an exceptional tailoring department), TVs, boys' clothes and Boy Scout and school uniforms. On four, you would find furniture, carpets, some high-end brands and fabric. The beauty shop was located there, as well. In the basement, markdowns and sale items were sold, in addition to work clothes and luggage. The basement level served briefly as a grocery store. The shoe repair shop was located there, too, as well as ladies' markdowns.

From the first floor, you could climb the stairs or take the elevator, one of four in the building, to the mezzanine level, where you could break for lunch at the Tea Room. Lunch items were on the menu, and a favorite was roast beef with coleslaw. The great part about the mezzanine level was that it was a balcony where you could watch eager shoppers move about the store. The Hub decorated for the seasons, and the windows were a destination, especially to see how designer Betty Richie decorated them for Christmas. Santa would arrive on the third floor, and after you gave him your list of Christmas presents, you were awarded with a little pink or blue gift of your own featuring a toy to hold you over. After the big day, December 26 was usually very busy with returns and sale giftwrap and cards. It was busy, as long as it wasn't a Sunday. The Hub was never open on a Sunday.

View of the east side of the 200 block of South Fourth Street in 1934. Morley's Clothes and Wilson's Drug Store were popular stores of the day. *Jefferson County Historical Association.*

By the mid-1960s, the Fort Steuben Mall was being built, and that provided bigger stores, better hours and plenty of parking. The Hub was only open two nights a week, and parking was often a concern. By the late 1960s, the Hub had purchased lots on Fifth Street, including the old Paramount Theater, and demolished them to make room for parking. In 1974, the Fort Steuben Mall opened, featuring Sears, Kaufmann's and, in 1975, Carlisle's. Eventually, sixty-five stores would occupy that space.

The Hub was on the decline and, in 1969, merged with L.S. Good; the name was changed in 1978. In 1980, the store closed, and that marked the end of an era. The building sat empty and neglected and was eventually torn down in 1993. A common item in local antique shops is a commemorative glass block from one of the many windows of the old building. Today, Dollar General occupies the spot at Fifth and Market where so many memories were made. It's hard to imagine that this was the location of the stately Hub department store, at one time the largest department store in the United States in a town of less than forty thousand residents. It's gone but very much not forgotten.

Concerts

For many summers while I was in college, I worked out at Star Lake in Burgettstown as a ticket taker. At that time, it was called the Post-Gazette Pavilion. Now, in its most recent rebranding, I am glad to see it being called the Pavilion at Star Lake while embracing its history once again. Being a ticket taker was possibly one of the best summer jobs I ever had. After the show started and the tickets were collected, there really wasn't much to do until the end of the show, when we had to stop—mostly inebriated—visitors from making off with the facility's rental chairs. The group of folks who worked in that department in those days were wonderful and on concert days would all bring a covered dish to share. During the downtime, we were often permitted to walk down to the stage and watch the show for a bit. During my time there, I saw Dave Matthews, Steve Miller, Tom Petty, Kiss, Ozzy Osborne and Joe Cocker, just to name just a few.

Looking back, Steubenville has played host to many well-known acts over the years. Attempting to make any sort of list of performers is very difficult; there are so many bands, clubs, restaurants and dancehalls where groups would perform that any attempt at compiling a complete list would be monumental. Also, in the online databases I use, some records are scant,

Façade of the Capitol Theatre showing the 1934 film *Here Comes the Navy*. *Jefferson County Historical Association.*

especially from the 1940s. So one must rely on the memories of friends, coworkers and family members who attended the shows or at least remember the groups coming to town.

The biggest reason musical groups came to Steubenville in the early years was the fact that Pennsylvania, specifically Pittsburgh, had what are known as "blue laws" on the books, which prohibited entertainment establishments from holding programs on Sundays, among other things. So, when national acts booked gigs in Pittsburgh—for instance, at the Stanley Theater, now the Benedum Center for the Performing Arts—on a Saturday, they would travel one hour west to Steubenville on Sunday to play, typically at the magnificent Capitol Theatre.

The Capitol hosted "the top big bands, radio personalities and movie stars," according to Dr. John Holmes in his book, *Remembering Steubenville*. Holmes lists several big band greats who played there, such as Duke Ellington, Glenn Miller, the Andrews Sisters, Ella Fitzgerald and Lena Horn, among others. In February 1940, bandleader Benny Goodman performed a live show there with his orchestra. From July 3–9, 1942, Tommy Dorsey opened at the Stanley for a weeklong engagement, and expectations were high that he would break the house record for attendance. On Sunday, July 5, he played Steubenville's Capitol Theatre for his weekly Sunday night radio program sponsored by the U.S. Treasury Department. Dorsey, in those days, also employed Frank Sinatra and Jo Stafford as singers, who most likely made the trip to Steubenville. Others who performed there were Sammy Kaye, Artie Shaw and Harry James, and my grandmother remembers seeing Cab Calloway—all performers at the Capitol.

By the 1960s, the laws prohibiting Sunday entertainment had been repealed, ending the necessity for bands to look for Sunday venues. That being said, Steubenville still attracted some great artists. The 1961 season in Steubenville seemed to be particularly exciting, with many shows held at the new Diocesan Community Arena. Buddy Morrow and his Night Train Orchestra appeared there in September, followed by Johnny Mathis. The Brothers Four performed in October. Undoubtedly, they played their hit

Aerial view of the 1957 grand opening of Frank and Jerry Furniture and Appliance, located at 122 North Fifth Street. The Paramount Theater is at left, and the Hub is at right. *Jerry Barilla.*

song "Greenfields," which was released the previous year. Also in October, the Supremes took the stage, followed by the Woody Herman Orchestra. In November, Bobby Rydell played with Bobby Vinton, a Canonsburg native. Vinton was in Steubenville more than once, playing at different venues. In February 1962, Chubby Checker appeared here with Bobby Comstock and the Counts.

Others who performed in Steubenville over the years included bandleaders Eddy Duchin, Gene Krupa, José Feliciano, Lionel Hampton and the "Polka King of Chicago," Li'l Wally, and his Famous Polka Band. One performance remembered fondly was given by "Godfather of Soul" James Brown—truly a show worth seeing.

More local bands also were in demand, like the 006's, People's Choice, Universal Joint, Crack the Sky, the Fantasy's and B.E. Taylor. The locally founded but nationally known group Wild Cherry, with Mingo native Rob Parissi, made it big with their 1976 hit "Play That Funky Music"—still a favorite in our area. And who can forget our native son, the "King of Cool" Dean Martin, born Dino Paul Crocetti right here in 1917?

TASTY HISTORY

The people of the Ohio Valley have contributed greatly to history both nationally and locally. From the mills that supplied the steel to win world wars, to professional athletes competing in a variety of sports, the people of the Ohio Valley have excelled. This is also true in food history. The Ohio Valley is not unique in the fact that many ethnic groups came to the area due to the steel industry, but the food culture that specifically grew out of this mix is unique. For example, according to the West Virginia Encyclopedia, a part of the West Virginia Humanities Council, the pepperoni roll was a delicacy developed by Italian immigrants around 1927 in the coal fields of northern West Virginia as a lunch for miners. This was an easy meal combining pepperoni, bread and cheese into a compact, handheld snack that was unique to the region. The necessity for an easy lunch for the hardworking coal miners led to this foodways innovation.

For most of us in the Ohio Valley, pepperoni rolls are a staple—and one that I had no idea was unique to this area until I left for college and was among folks from other parts of the country. Another staple that is unique to our valley and is gaining popularity nationwide is what they call Ohio Valley Pizza, Steubenville-Style or what we know simply as DiCarlo's Pizza. For my family growing up, there was no other pizza we would get. This style of pizza is totally unique to our area. According to the history on its website, DiCarlo's started as a grocery store in Steubenville operated by Italian immigrants Michael and Caroline DiCarlo and their six children. After their oldest son, Primo, returned to Steubenville after serving in World War II, he brought back a new dish he saw in Italy called pizza. The DiCarlos' first pizza shop opened in Steubenville in 1945 and was in the 100 block of South Third, near the fort today. This was the first pizza shop to open in Steubenville. According to an article that appeared in the *Herald-Star* in January 2015, Primo DiCarlo, grandson of the founder, recounted that this first shop was the very first retail pizza shop in Ohio. By 1949, Primo's brother, Galdo, had become a partner, and they opened a pizza shop in Wheeling. In 1951, the Sunset Boulevard location opened, and by the late 1950s, twenty-four shops were open in the Ohio Valley. In 1977, the original Third Street store closed, and a new building was built on Adams Street. Today, DiCarlo's Pizza has extended from Ohio and West Virginia to Pennsylvania and South Carolina.

Looking west on Market Street in Steubenville. Woolworth's, a popular five-and-ten store, was located on the corner. *Jefferson County Historical Association.*

What makes this pizza so unique is the thick crust, the homemade sauce and the cheese added after it comes out of the oven. To me and my family, this pizza just tastes like home. I am also proud to say that my wife, an Italian girl from Brooklyn, has embraced this pizza as well, and that is high praise, if you ask me.

Another Ohio Valley staple that is not necessarily unique to this area is the Italian cookie known as the pizzelle. The pizzelle was brought over with Italian immigrants in the early twentieth century. The egg-based batter mixes flour and sugar, among other things, in addition to the flavor of your choice, such as vanilla, lemon, orange or anise. I prefer anise seed to anise oil. The batter must be the right consistency to cook in a pizzelle iron, similar to a waffle iron but much thinner. The way that these were made in the old days was to employ a bulky and heavy pizzelle iron on a pole that one had to hold

Fort Steuben Bridge, built in 1928, looking toward West Virginia. To the left is the Half-Moon area and a Mail-Pouch Tobacco barn in the distance. *Weirton Area Museum and Cultural Center.*

over a range, being careful not to burn themselves. To Steubenville resident Charles "Chip" DeMarco, there had to be a better way. In the 1950s, Charles invented the electric pizzelle iron in his shop called Tri-State Machine and Driveshaft. Charles and his wife, Helen, then patented the invention and began selling it all over the country. Helen would also demonstrate the iron in department stores like the Hub in downtown Steubenville. From 1959 to 1969, Charles sold his pizzelle iron around the country, making the process of cooking the pizzelle much easier and faster. Personally, the electric pizzelle iron has been a big part of my upbringing. I have fond memories of my dad and grandfather sitting at the kitchen table making pizzelle around the holiday seasons, specifically Easter and Christmas. Being old enough to operate the iron was like a rite of passage in my house, and I looked forward to the day that I could take up the reins. I, like so many folks who make the tasty treat, have Steubenville's own Charles DeMarco to thank.

The people of the Ohio Valley have always been innovators. Our unique foodways and traditions have impacted not only our region but also our nation, from the pepperoni roll, to pizza, to the pizzelle. Our history is pretty delicious!

Chapter 4

WEIRTON AND HANCOCK COUNTY

Anyone who knows me will already be aware of my love for Williamsburg in Virginia. As a historian, Williamsburg was like Disneyland to me. The experience of visiting a place with so much history and a living sense of the past is captivating. Luckily for me, that feeling has generally stayed with me all these years. I am fortunate that in an old space, be it a house, battlefield or on a city street, I can almost feel the past. I don't believe in ghosts as specters that haunt the living, but I do believe that memory can leave an imprint on a space. Whether that imprint is something measurable, or perhaps something internal, is up for debate. That could also just be the personality of a hopeless nostalgic at heart, but I also find that you don't always need to be in the presence of a historic place to feel its history.

With all that said, when I can connect our local history to early Virginia, I get excited. For West Virginia, our early history *is* Virginia history. West Virginia was created on June 20, 1863, born out of the struggles of the Civil War. The war was a clinching point in a long line of issues plaguing the people who lived in the western counties of the Old Dominion. One issue among many in the creation of the new state of West Virginia was the distance between the western counties and the seat of government in Richmond. The distance was just too far in an era of horse-drawn vehicles and unimproved roads through the mountains. The railroad helped later, but the folks in the Northern Panhandle of West Virginia would have quite the journey to the statehouse.

It was in that same vein—in the matter of distance, one must travel to do business—that the idea of Hancock County came about. All the area encompassing Hancock and Brooke Counties in West Virginia, Westmoreland and parts of Allegheny, Beaver, Washington and Fayette Counties in Pennsylvania, including the current site of Pittsburgh, were once part of a vast county called Yohogania County, Virginia. This county was formed in 1776 from the District of West Augusta. Two other counties were formed from the district at the same time, those being Ohio and Monongalia Counties in Virginia. As one can imagine, there were quite a number of disputes between Virginia and Pennsylvania regarding this land, citing land patents and treaties on both sides of the issue going back to the kings of England in the seventeenth century.

During the American Revolution, in December 1779, the Second Continental Congress basically put a stop to the fighting between the states and urged them to come to a solution. To put it simply, the border of the Northern Panhandle was agreed on and laid out, finally, in 1784. The County of Yohogania ceased to exist after only seven years, when it was determined, based on the survey between the states of Virginia and Pennsylvania, that most of the county was contained in Pennsylvania. The remaining part of the county that remained in Virginia, present-day Hancock and Brooke Counties, was then absorbed into Ohio County. The annexation was short-lived because in 1796, Ohio County divided, creating Brooke County, basically encompassing that remaining part of the original Yohogania County.

By the 1840s, there were disputes about the distance one must travel from the northern end of Brooke County down to Wellsburg, which was the county seat. There was talk about moving the county seat to Holliday's Cove, now part of downtown Weirton, to be more centrally located, but due to the overwhelming population in the southern part of Brooke County, traction could not be made to move the seat of government. Something had to be done. In 1846, a New Manchester resident and surveyor named Thomas Bambrick was elected to the Virginia legislature from Brooke County. He could be regarded as the father of Hancock County. An immigrant, Bambrick came to the United States in 1815 from his home in County Kilkenny, Ireland. Having prepared to become a Roman Catholic priest, Bambrick was well educated, and on immigrating to Brooke County, he became a teacher, tutor and bookkeeper for the residents of the northern end of the county. Assuming his position in the Virginia legislature, Bambrick quickly presented legislation to form a new county from Brooke. The

The Griffith House was an early blockhouse that served as a home fortification for area settlers in the event of Native American attacks. This building was demolished to make way for the Weir High School stadium in downtown Weirton. *Weirton Area Museum and Cultural Center.*

Virginia legislature passed the resolution on January 15, 1848, and allowed Bambrick to choose the name of the new county. Due to his admiration of the first signer of the Declaration of Independence, John Hancock, Hancock County was chosen.

Jack Welch, in his book *History of Hancock County*, relates most of this history. My favorite story about the surveying of the border between the two counties is contained in this text. The issue of the border stems from the fact that both counties wanted control of the tollhouse that was located on Pittsburgh Pike at the juncture of Cove and Colliers Roads. Welsh writes, "The line was to be surveyed from a point on the Ohio River, at what was known as Williams Rocks to a point joining the PA boarder. Mr. Bambrick met the surveyors as they were approaching the site…and suggested a trip to Steubenville. There he staged a party for them. Later in the day when they departed for Williams Rocks, they began at a point slightly south of the original point, thus giving Hancock County possession of the toll house."

Early records of Hancock County are interesting to read, as they give the statistics of the new county. Looking at taxable personal property in the county in 1848, there were 968 horses, 12 gold watches, 82 silver watches, 157 metal clocks, 236 wooden clocks and 64 jerseys, pianos and carriages. There was also one enslaved person, who in 1848 was considered taxable property. That number increased to three in 1850 and was reduced to two by 1860. In that year, the rumblings of civil war could be felt even in such an isolated place as Hancock County. In June 1861, a vote for secession was called, and only 23 residents voted to leave the Union, while 743 voted to remain. It seems that the residents of this area identified more with their neighboring states then they did with the factions in Richmond. All of this served to further the divide the state of Virginia and led to the creation of West Virginia in 1863.

Our history is tied to Virginia, and there are quite a few reminders left here that bind our roots deep in the Old Dominion. This area, once the subject of conversations in the halls of the Second Continental Congress, has come a long way from the vast county of Yohogania. There is history in these hills, if you know where to look.

A Senator's House

It seems appropriate that I wrote this book in the form of biweekly columns for the newspaper originally, because that is also where I discovered my own passion for working in museums. Many years ago, while reading the paper, I encountered an appeal for volunteers for a newly created local museum located in New Cumberland, West Virginia. At that time, the Hancock County Historical Museum had recently purchased the Marshall House on Ridge Avenue in New Cumberland for the purpose of creating a county museum. As someone who habitually visited museums and historic houses and sites with my family, I was eager to help out at my local museum. So, on the set night, my grandmother and I ventured out for the informational meeting, and the rest is history.

The Marshall House is a survivor from the last quarter of the nineteenth century. It has stood at 1008 Ridge Avenue since it was completed in 1887. The builder, Oliver Sheridan Marshall, was a successful lawyer and politician.

Incredibly, most of his law books can still be found in his study on the first floor of his home. An 1878 graduate of Bethany College, Marshall returned to Hancock County to serve as the principal of New Cumberland Grade School until 1885. His first position in government was in 1884,

View of Senator Oliver S. Marshall standing in a 1913 Buick at the home opener of the 1915 Weirton baseball season. The Weirton Athletic Association took on the Steubenville Berkshire team. *Weirton Area Museum and Cultural Center.*

when he was elected clerk of the County Court of Hancock County; later, in 1896, he was elected to the West Virginia senate. In 1899, he even served as president of the senate, and his home reflects a man in that position. The stately, five-bedroom home is richly appointed in the Queen Anne style popular in the 1880s. The first floor is adorned with cherrywood, hardwood floors, a stained-glass window, interior shutters and original fireplace mantels. The floor plan is slightly quirky, even for the time in which it was built. The story goes that Oliver S. Marshall's first wife, Elizabeth Tarr, loved the Ohio River and wished to be able to see it from every room. Elizabeth Tarr was the great-granddaughter of Peter Tarr, proprietor of the furnace on Kings Creek. Her father, Campbell, was a successful merchant from Wellsburg and a delegate from Brooke County elected as a Unionist at the 1861 Virginia Secession Convention. This meeting was held in Richmond to discuss whether Virginia would leave the Union in the din before the Civil War. Campbell voted against all calls for secession and was expelled from the session due to that fact.

Later, Campbell joined the movement for the creation for the new state of West Virginia and served as the state's first treasurer from 1863 to 1867. Elizabeth married Oliver in 1880, and they enjoyed seven years together. She had a hand in the building of their home in New Cumberland, but sadly didn't live long enough to enjoy it, passing away the same year the house was completed. Born to this union were Olive and John Marshall. As the couple's only children when the home was built, their names were etched in the transoms above their respective rooms.

In 1904, Olive died at only eighteen, devastating her father tremendously. John went on to graduate and later serve on the Board of Trustees of Bethany College. In 1925, he was appointed the assistant attorney general under President Calvin Coolidge, a position he held until 1929. He passed away in 1966. Oliver went on to marry Nora Householder in 1890 and have three more children, Edith, Edmund and Virginia. Oliver passed away in 1934, and Nora followed in 1952. Virginia Marshall never married but lived a very full life working as a teacher in New Cumberland for forty years. Miss Marshall, as she was affectionately known, lived to be ninety-nine years old while still remaining in her childhood home. As the story goes, she wanted the house to be torn down after her death, as she couldn't bear it falling into disrepair or worse. I never had the pleasure of meeting Miss Marshall, but I would like to think that she would be honored to know her family home is the site of a museum.

Today, the Marshall House is full of history, not just the history of the Marshall family but that of the county, too, and its importance in state, local and national history. It is an appropriate choice for the county museum, as the family's history can be traced to our early pioneers, connects to the Civil War and West Virginia history and exemplifies domestic life in a small town at the turn of the twentieth century. Due to the Marshalls' long tenure in the old home, some of the family's possessions are still retained, my favorite being two field hockey sticks found in the cavernous attic. I imagine on rainy days, the Marshall children would play up there to stay out of the grown-ups' way. Maybe John would creep down and listen to his father talk law in his study. Perhaps this is where he was inspired to practice law himself in later life. I know the house and its story inspired me, more than one hundred years later, to follow my passion and pursue a career in the museum field. So, pick up that paper, take a chance and volunteer. You never know where it will lead you.

A VIRGINIA MAP

Sometimes one comes across something that is too good to pass up. As a collector, despite what my bank account tells me, some things are just too good to be true. And if you can't purchase whatever it is that you wanted to buy, a story about it quickly follows. I have many stories that begin with, "One time I was at an antique store, and I saw such and such, but I had no money…" You will never forget those stories, and if you continue to frequent those sorts of establishments, you will always be on the lookout.

On my seemingly ever-growing list of collectables, I like to look for pictures, paintings and old maps. My wife and I reserve one wall in our house for the pictures we've most recently purchased, and that keeps things interesting for us. While perusing the internet recently for something new to add to our gallery wall, I stumbled on the Library of Congress's map collection, which includes a digital collection. I have used this site in the past for other things, but this time, I stumbled on a map I had never seen before. The map in question is of Hancock County, Virginia, from 1852. At this time, the county had recently split from Brooke County. I spent a lot of time looking at this old map against a current map to see what has changed, and as one can imagine, there is a lot to talk about.

In 1852, the railroads had not yet come into our area; that development would come a few years later and would open our area up, like so many others, to the world. The main thoroughfare through the southern end of the county was the Holliday's Cove and Pittsburgh Turnpike. This road had a tollhouse, and in Holliday's Cove, there was at least one tavern, according to historian Mary Shakley Ferguson. The road passed through Weirton along more or less same route as Main Street going north, until it reached Cove Road. It then followed that road until it turned left up the hill across from where Weirton Lumber is today following the current route. According to the map, if you were riding on that road toward Pennsylvania in 1852, before you arrived at Holliday's Cove, you would go through an area called Danville. Going through the town, you may have turned left up the hill at what is today Weir Avenue and Cove Road and joined South Eleventh Street toward the hilltop. Surprisingly, those sections of roads were here in the 1850s. To the left and below what is today Weir Avenue, there was a creek called Griffiths Run that flowed toward Harmon Creek, as well.

Going up Cove Road Hill from where Weirton Lumber is today, you would have passed through a section of town called Demopolis. Following the road and a telegraph line, one would pass Greenbrier Road along Bear

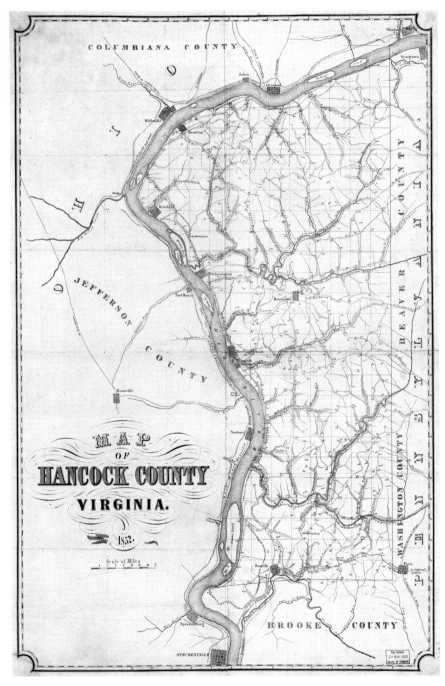

Map of Hancock County, Virginia, published in 1852. *Library of Congress.*

Run on the left. The next run one would come to going up the hill would be Skull Run. This valley is located to the left of where Nick's Towing is now located. I would love to find out how Skull Run got its name. Both Skull and Bear Run flow into Roberts Run, which is to the right of Cove Road as you ascend the hill; it, too, flows into Harmons Creek.

Today, if one were to follow South Eleventh Street, the road would wind over the hilltop, cross Pennsylvania Avenue and descend into a valley on what is today South Twelfth Street. In 1852, this road existed and followed what was know then as Sugar Tree Run. When you reached Kings Creek, there would be quite a few roads to travel. There appears to have been another road descending the hillside from what is today Weirton Heights joining the intersection by where Willow Street intersects South Twelfth Street. Today, that road is gone, but looking at Google Maps, I surmise that this road could have connected to what is today the end of North Twentieth Street. Since the oldest house in the county, the circa 1785 Truax House, is just off that street, it would make sense that North Twentieth was a busier thoroughfare and led to Kings Creek at one time. There was a crossing at Kings Creek at that point, as there is today, and the road wound up to the intersection of North Fork and Hudson Hill Roads; that's where this part of Kings Creek Road stopped. According to the map, there was another crossing in that area near the end of Willow Street that crossed the creek onto the grounds of what is today the Serbian Picnic Grounds. Today, 169 years later, that part of the road is long gone. A road matching the route of Kings Creek Road picks up again and travels east and crosses the creek into what is today Country Club Estates, avoiding the sharp curve near the entrance to Lick Run. That road had its own creek, crossing which is the bridge at the end of today's Culler Road. Going up Culler Road, the road in 1852 followed what was known then as Parks Run and, later, Charcoal Run, which today is the little run on the left as you drive up the hill. Around where Bass Drive is today, the 1852 road separates from the current route and travels to the left up the valley and to connect to Pennsylvania Avenue somewhere near where Starvaggi Drive is today. At the juncture of Culler and Kings Creek Roads, there appears to be another road that goes through Country Club Estates and up over the hill connecting to what is today either Shady Avenue or Pleasantview Drive and joining the current route of Culler Road back toward Pennsylvania Avenue, joining to it where Gio's is today.

All in all, I would think that if you were dropped in our area in 1852, you might be able to navigate with a fair amount of accuracy, given that most of the routes were the same then as they are today. But if someone told you to

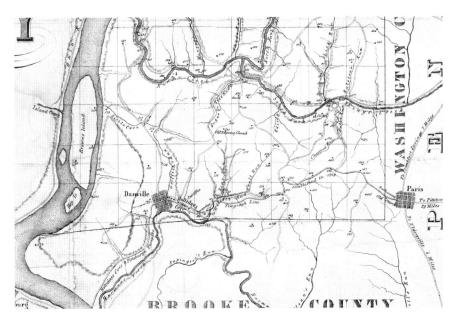

Detail of Holliday's Cove showing roads, waterways and houses. From a 1852 map of Hancock County, Virginia. *Library of Congress.*

pass Skull Run on the road to Demopolis, you might have some trouble. This map was, to me, too good to pass up, and the information gleaned from it is a snapshot into our history. So next time you ride on South Eleventh Street or down Culler Road, look for the ghosts of the past around you on these antique thoroughfares.

CRAWFORD'S CROSSING

Ask any student of history what the one thing they wish they could go back in time and experience from the past is, and I bet you would have some pretty cool answers. For me, it could be witnessing the excitement of V-E Day after so many years at war. For my wife it is witnessing Washington crossing the Delaware during the American Revolution. I know that there are places in our community that would have been worth seeing, as well. I would love to have seen our valley before the mills came, especially the area of North Weirton, which, at the time before Weir bought it, was all still farmland, owned since 1902 by a fellow called Cyrus Ferguson.

According to David Javersak, who wrote *The History of Weirton*, it was Ferguson who was initially responsible for bringing industry to our valley

Corner of Lee Avenue and Main Street in Weirton. The First Christian Church is at the far right. *Weirton Area Museum and Cultural Center.*

and selling part of his landholdings to E.T. Weir. One place I would love to have seen is the Ferguson home, also known as the Crawford Mansion. The mansion was located on Pennsylvania Avenue in downtown Weirton in the lot to the right of the old post office and across the street from the former Bank of Weirton, now the home of the Weirton Covenant Church. Crawford Avenue at the east end of that block is named in honor of that family. This rambling home was built around 1849 by Robert Crawford. It was sprawling, two stories high, with a large front porch and a large side porch to the left of the building.

Robert was born in Donegal, Ireland, in 1799 and came to this country around 1820. By 1821, Crawford had settled near Pittsburgh in the Saw Mill Run area just south of the city. He bought and sold land in that area for about twenty years, owning many lots and interests in the South Hills area of Pittsburgh. In 1824, Crawford applied for American citizenship, which the Supreme Court of Pennsylvania granted him in 1826. A clever and successful businessman, Crawford expanded his business enterprises by acquiring ferries and facilitating trade up and down the river. Business in the Pittsburgh area was good, and Crawford continued to have interests there at least until 1866. The financial panic of 1837, though, may have enticed him to move his enterprises south. John Crawford, one of Robert's brothers, had come to America around 1819 and settled on Kings Creek. Possibly John introduced Robert to this area, because around 1843, Robert purchased 231 acres of land in the area, eventually owning 549 acres in total by 1856.

It was quite exciting when the Crawford family moved to the area from the big city. Mary Ferguson recounts in her book *The History of Hollidays Cove*, "On Sunday morning they created quite a stir driving down the valley in their surrey, with the fringe on the top, to attend services. Mrs. Crawford and her daughters, right out of Pittsburgh, wore the very latest in bonnets, capes, silks and satins. They were something to be envied and emulated by local females; and made it quite worth the while for the faithless to start attending church again."

Robert did not stay on the farm long. By 1857, he had turned over management of the farm to his son John Crawford and John's new wife, Mary Porter of New Cumberland. Robert moved to Steubenville, where he had purchased property, and became a prominent citizen there. Although his father still owned the family farm in Virginia, John and Mary had seven children in the Crawford Mansion homestead, five of whom survived into adulthood. Shortly after the house was built, a stone barn was constructed nearby. It was said that Enoch Davis was the carpenter for both the home

Postcard view of the Weirton Post Office located on Pennsylvania Avenue across from the Mill Administration Building, or MAB. *Author's collection.*

Cove Presbyterian Church, dedicated in January 1861 in Holliday's Cove. The current church building was erected on the same spot. *Weirton Area Museum and Cultural Center.*

The Crawford House, built in 1849 by Robert Crawford. The home was located to the right of the Weirton Post Office on Pennsylvania Avenue. *Weirton Area Museum and Cultural Center.*

and the barn. George Pentecost completed the stonework for $1,000, but on the night he received payment for his work, he lost it all playing euchre.

John Crawford owned a piano at his home and was an avid violin player. He was also choir director and an elder at Cove Presbyterian Church. During the Civil War, John was a staunch supporter of the United States, and when Virginia voted to leave the Union in 1861, he, along with a sizeable contingent of prominent Hancock County men, went to Wheeling in May to discuss creating a restored government in Virginia. Later that year, in July, John enlisted in the Panhandle Greys and became a first lieutenant. This group, which at its height in 1862 consisted of fifty-nine men, was a local militia made up of men who formed a home guard to protect the community from possible raiding and guerilla warfare by the Confederacy in our area. They came together for about nine days a month for "service." Requests were made from the group several times for rifles and ammunition from the restored government, but none were sent. The men of the Panhandle Greys had to be content to use old muskets to defend their homes. No fighting came to this area during the Civil War, so the home guard was not called into service.

John and his family were very prominent in the community after the Civil War. In 1870, old Robert Crawford died in Steubenville and was buried in Union Cemetery. Shortly before his death, he officially gave the

OCT 1958

The Crawford family stone barn, pictured in 1958. This building was later used as a city garage for Weirton. Legend has it that a tunnel connected the house and barn and was a stop on the Underground Railroad. *Weirton Area Museum and Cultural Center*.

farm to his son, who took great care of his holdings, which by that time were nearing 623 acres. While working on that farm in 1885, John injured himself due to a splinter under his fingernail. The wound became infected, and John contracted lockjaw, today known as tetanus. It was not treated in time, and John passed away at the age of fifty-five. He is interred at Three Springs Cemetery. Mary went on living at the mansion, selling off parts of the farm in 1887 to the railroad, establishing Crawford's Crossing. In 1902, she sold off the farm to Cyrus Ferguson. Mary passed away in 1919 at the age of eighty-six.

In the ensuing years, the city of Weirton grew up around the place, and the old barn was used as the city garage. For many years, it was thought that there was a tunnel connecting the house and the barn that could have been part of the Underground Railroad, and although evidence was recently found on the site to confirm the story, descendants of the Crawford family, speaking in the 1960s, refuted the claims. The barn was demolished in 1961, and the house soon followed in 1965. Today, there is nothing left on the site except a vacant lot. Perhaps if you listen closely in that empty space, you may be able to hear the sound of the home guard marching on the front lawn or the the piano playing in the grand rooms of the lost Crawford Mansion. I hear it; do you?

CYRUS FERGUSON

I love to read about our local history, specifically the time when our area moved from rural to urban or, rather, industrial. I find it fascinating to see the huge technological shift from our agrarian society to a more industrial way of life. Thinking about my own generation and how we grew up versus that of my children is staggering, let alone my grandparents' generation versus my children's. I think the most incredible generation for leaps in technological innovations would be that of the late nineteenth century through the mid-twentieth century. For me, it is mind-boggling to think that one could be born into an agrarian society with horses and buggies, oil lamps and outhouses and leave this world in a time of automobiles, electricity and television.

The Industrial Revolution, typically a topic one learns about in school, came about in the nineteenth century. As with any momentous event in our history, there were good and bad outcomes as a result of the change. For us in our valley, industry came to dominate, thus largely replacing the rural way of life here. In Steubenville especially, industry came pretty early in the nineteenth century. The advent of the foundries, woolen factories and other manufactories propelled Steubenville to the forefront of progress at that time. Its neighbor across the river, Holliday's Cove, West Virginia, in Hancock County, remained relatively rural in the nineteenth century—that is, until a man bought up most of the farms in the area with the dream of establishing an industry and a community. No, it's not who you think; E.T. Weir didn't come to Weirton until 1909. The man who brought industry to Holliday's Cove was Cyrus Ferguson.

Now almost forgotten, Cyrus Ferguson was responsible for most of our industry in Weirton. Without him, it is plausible that the officials of Weirton Steel would not have been able to purchase the ground for their new mills. Also, the workforce would not have been able to venture from Steubenville to staff the factories. Cyrus Ferguson is as important to our area as any of our early industrialists.

According to Jack Welch's 1963 book *History of Hancock County*, Cyrus was born on September 20, 1851, on what was then the David Campbell farm, about two miles east of Weirton on the brick road leading to Paris, Pennsylvania. Cyrus's father went west in 1849 during the California Gold Rush, and both of his parents died when Cyrus was still young. After the death of his parents, Cyrus spent most of his childhood working on various farms in Hancock County. In 1875, Cyrus married Mary Elizabeth Smith, and they went on to have six children. Cyrus opened a meat market in Wellsburg around 1883, and in 1885, he moved his young family to McDonald, Pennsylvania, where he established a brickworks and meat market in that city. He was also a founding member, in 1892, of the Ferguson Hose Company, a group of volunteer firemen in McDonald. Around that same time, he entered the oil business in McDonald, which greatly increased his wealth.

In 1902, Cyrus returned to Holliday's Cove and purchased 1,700 acres of land, most of what is today modern downtown Weirton, and set up a homestead at the old Crawford mansion, located at the corner of Crawford and Pennsylvania Avenues. According to Jack Welch, "In 1907 Ferguson discovered and developed the prolific Holliday's Cove oil pool, situated on both sides of the Panhandle railroad and just east of the Holliday's Cove depot, extending for over three miles to the top of the hill above Wheeling Junction. This deposit was one of the largest Bereagrit sand oil pools ever discovered in the world." In 1908, the Holliday's Cove Oil pool produced over six thousand barrels of oil a day, but this output steadily declined as that year went on. According to Lewis Truax in his manuscript "My Life Story as I Have Seen Weirton Grow," there was an oil boom here between 1885 and 1915. "The Hudson brothers were very famous at that time because they had a great amount of oil well machinery and drilling equipment. That is why the road is called Hudson Hill Road because it goes through the Dave Hudson farm at the foot of the hill. The oil fields provided a very great amount of work for the farmers. A great many used their teams of horses for hauling the machinery and equipment to and from the wells." Truax remembers Cyrus's oil derricks "around his farm two on the hillside above the High School Stadium (old Jimmy Carey Stadium downtown), two or three above where the city building is now, where the old Atlantic Service station was." Before that, though, according to Mary Ferguson in her book *The History of Holliday's Cove*, "the first well drilled in the cove was on the banks of Harmon Creek above the old Cove Station. It was drilled with a spring pole using man power. They drilled some 300 feet but they struck only sand. No one knew at that time, that a depth of 1,500 feet was required to reach oil in this vicinity. A well came in on the Robert Patterson Place on the hill across from Three Springs Cemetery, on the present Woodland Estates, and it produced 60 barrels a day."

Cyrus Ferguson took advantage of the discovery of oil and drilled his property from Weirton to Follansbee. Due to his successes, he became Holliday's Cove's first millionaire. Jack Welch recounts that in 1909, E.T. Weir bought 105 acres from Cyrus Ferguson in what would be known as North Weirton, the land that would become the Weirton Steel Company. Eventually, Weir would purchase over 1,200 acres from Ferguson. Cyrus, even after the sale to E.T. Weir, still had extensive holdings in the Weirton area, but he didn't just provide land for big industry, though. "In 1912

View of North Weirton soon after the community was settled in 1909. *Weirton Area Museum and Cultural Center.*

he laid out his first allotment of 160 lots extending from Virginia Ave to Purdys Alley and Main Street," Welch adds. "Mr. Ferguson threw his energy into the building of the valley, giving free factory sites to bring in Weirton's industries, donating lots for the building of various schoolhouses and churches in Weirton, and taking a leading part in securing improvement in the community." Ferguson also was a principal in the construction of the Market Street Bridge in 1905, which linked Steubenville with West Virginia.

Later in his life, Cyrus relocated west to Colorado and Wyoming, where he owned vast landholdings, perhaps to escape the industry he helped create. In 1926, he passed away in Denver, and his remains were removed to Union Cemetery in Steubenville. His wife, Mary, passed away in 1940.

Cyrus was instrumental in bringing industry to our valley. It was a time when our rural past met with our industrial future. Without him, the valley's history would be drastically different.

SUGAR CAMP HOLLOW

One of my favorite books growing up was a children's book by West Virginia resident and Weirton native Anna Egan Smucker. Her book *No Star Night* was enchanting and one I personally resonated with, since it takes place in town. The book is still in print, and I encourage anyone who grew up in our area in the 1950s to buy a copy and share it with their loved ones. Without spoiling it, the climax of the story takes place in what we call the Slag Dump.

This area is located just off Pennsylvania Avenue on the right as one drives up Weirton Heights Hill from downtown Weirton. As a child, I remember steam or smoke coming off the hills, and I recently learned that it is from water reacting with the acid in the slag, a byproduct of the steel-making process. What was interesting to me—as Anna Egan Smucker references in her story—is that the great big mountain of slag was not always a great big mountain but a deep valley called Sugar Camp Hollow.

Sugar Camp Hollow, or rather its destruction, is referenced in a few local history books, most notably *The History of Holliday's Cove* by Mary Shakley Ferguson. Ferguson writes, "Beautiful Sugar Camp Hollow, where service-berry, dogwood and Judas trees came out to say spring is here is silent. The mouth of this hollow was once a picnic ground where children played in the stream that tumbled down from the hollow, men played softball on the lower level, and women dipped water from the spring that bubbled from the hillside to make coffee." I am not sure if Sugar Camp Hollow was a park

Postcard view of North Weirton at the intersection of Pennsylvania Avenue and Main Street. Weirton Steel's administration building, the open-hearth furnace, the Crawford barn and St. Paul's School can be seen. *Author's collection.*

or perhaps just a nice shady area where folks would come and enjoy nature. The name Sugar Camp also alludes to the fact that perhaps there was, in fact, a sugar camp and shack on the property there as well, but I haven't found a historical reference to corroborate that fact. I can appreciate, then, that the hollow must have had a fair amount of sugar maple trees. As an aside, this year, I tried my hand at producing maple syrup from a few of the sugar maple trees on our woodlot, with a varying amount of success. From four trees, I was able to produce about a quart of finished syrup. With a ratio of forty gallons of sap to create one gallon of syrup, I was pretty busy. It can be assumed that perhaps in Sugar Camp Hollow there was a boiling house or a "sugar shack," as they are colloquially known, to boil the liquid sap directly from the tree into maple syrup.

I am not sure when the first load of slag was dumped in Sugar Camp Hollow, but Mary Ferguson recalls that when it happened, the residents of Holliday's Cove and the new community of Weirton were not very pleased. Ferguson writes, "When the first load of slag was dumped into this hollow, the people screamed their resentment.…But they were promised the hollow was only being leveled for home sites and it would be even more beautiful." As we know, the piles of slag just grew, and the little valley became a towering hill.

Eventually, between 1910 and 1920, Weirton Heights was being developed, and a new road was needed to connect the community of Weirton and the mills to the new housing developments on the hilltops. Before 1914, the only way to access Weirton Heights was to use Cove Road or South Eleventh Street, or what we call Powerhouse Road. Louis Truax, in his manuscript about growing up in Weirton at the turn of the twentieth century, recalls fondly when Weirton Heights Hill was surveyed in 1913. The road was finished in 1914, with one lane brick and one slag. Pennsylvania Avenue would continue up the hill through Sugar Camp Hollow, which, according to Mary Ferguson, was previously only suitable for horse-drawn vehicles. The new road joined with what was known as Cemetery Road through Weirton Heights to connect to Cove Road, near the present-day fire station, and off to the state line.

The road was eventually widened and improved over many years, and the slag dump grew higher still. It was on this road, at the tight bend near the bottom of the hill and the P&W bus garage, that one of the worst tragedies in the city occurred. Over seventy years ago, on April 29, 1951, a packed P&W bus heading downtown carrying mostly churchgoers crashed into the concrete wall at the curve. The bus lost its brakes on the descent down the hill, and despite the courageous efforts of the bus driver, Joe Kraina, to stop the bus by turning up Angela Street, a little alley to the left of the bus

Mary Shakley Ferguson's painting of Christmas in Holliday's Cove in 1908. Cove Presbyterian Church is at left. *Roger Criss and Cove Presbyterian Church.*

Photograph of the Starvaggi Bus Garage at the bend of Pennsylvania Avenue, taken in 1948. This would later be the site of the April 1951 bus wreck in which fourteen were killed when a bus collided with the wall at the bend. *Weirton Area Museum and Cultural Center.*

garage, the vehicle collided with the concrete wall. The bus was carrying fifty-nine passengers. Of those on board, fourteen lost their lives, including the driver and my great-aunt Elizabeth Kaminski, who was twenty years old. Mary Zwierzchowski penned a concise account of the accident for the spring 2004 edition of *Goldenseal Magazine* called "An Easter Tragedy," writing poignantly of this event that was such a defining moment in our community.

Although the parklike setting is gone from Sugar Camp Hollow, the great trucks are no longer dumping slag on the hillside, either. The great mountain of slag is being quarried out for use elsewhere, and I think that would make the early residents of our area happy. It will take some time for the area to resemble a park again, and perhaps in some distant time in the future, a story will be written of the great slag hill that once stood where a lush valley is today.

Weirton Heights

There are clues to the past everywhere. Old buildings, roads, neighborhoods and areas or locations that have unique names but we can't remember why are fascinating to me. Weirton is a relatively young city compared to our neighbors Steubenville and Wellsburg. If you count Holliday's Cove, our area does date back to the eighteenth century, but remnants of the original eighteenth-century community are few and far between. In North Weirton, the unincorporated company town of Weirton sprang up in 1909 due to the mill opening in that area. The history of the communities on the hilltops are fascinating, as well.

I grew up on Weirton Heights and was always interested in how the community came to be. Surely, there was something there before the building booms of the early 1950s. Fortunately, I was a child right before home computers and video games were widely available, so for me, spending the day outside, meeting neighbors, helping with outside chores and exploring the neighborhood was the order of the day. Playing detective in my local woods, I soon discovered a row of neatly planted, fairly large black cherry trees and a few remaining evenly spaced hickory-log fence posts along the edge of a hillside, which at some point in the last seventy years had been the edge of a farmer's field. It's true that where I grew up, amid the neatly planned houses, not long ago there had been a farm. According to historian Louis Truax, who grew up when Weirton Heights was still a farming community, the William Ralston family had a farm at the top of Culler Road in the nineteenth century. Sometime around 1917, the area was sold to the Culler family. A good farmer, Hersel Culler kept livestock (which explained why I was able to find cow bones behind my parents' home) and had fruit trees. The area where Highview Circle is today was a lush apple orchard. Sometime in the 1940s, it was subdivided and sold off into lots.

Driving on up toward Pennsylvania Avenue, one will run into a promontory knoll with several houses on a short street called Crest Street, now near Auto Zone and the old osteopathic hospital. This small area was once known as Chestnut Woods. Before 1923, the American chestnut tree was a common variety in our local woods, but a blight swept the nation in the 1920s and all but killed the species. The trees in Chestnut Woods were huge, almost three feet in circumference, according to Truax. Across the street from Chestnut Woods was the White Farm, which encompassed the area where the Weirton Shopping Plaza is now and the area where St.

Joseph the Worker Church is. Near the top of the hill near Park Avenue was a little roadside park with a pavilion and picnic tables. It was a well-used community site.

From the Weirton Shopping Plaza to Starvaggi Drive was the Ed Blou Farm. Past that, encompassing all the area in Bel-Air addition, was the Joseph Miller Farm. On Colliers Way, the Gardner family had farms. Where Walgreens and Memorial Baptist Church are today was the Shipley Farm. And the Hindman Farm was where the area around Three Springs Drive is today. The area around where Three Springs Cemetery is now located was once a high hill, but due to mining, the ground surrounding the cemetery was drastically lowered and leveled out; this is the reason the cemetery is higher than the surrounding area. This proved a welcome space for Weirton's own airport, which operated in the flat land surrounding the cemetery.

Pennsylvania Avenue was paved with one lane brick and one lane slag in about 1913, starting with the intersection of County Road and Main Street downtown to the state line. Before this, folks had to use South Eleventh Street, sometimes called Powerhouse Road, or Lee Avenue Hill to go downtown. You could also use Cove Road or travel on Greenbrier Road. At the top of Greenbrier Road was the Campbell farm. According to Truax, in 1885, near that area, in a place known as Bear Den Hollow, the last bear was killed on Weirton Heights.

Most of the earliest housing developments on Weirton Heights began near the top of the hill near the Hancock County Sheltered Workshop in about 1913. As farmers left the fields and joined the men in the mills, the once-sweeping areas of open farm were subdivided and sold off. Other enterprises were being bult in Weirton Heights at that time. In 1916, a coal mine was built below the area behind what is today Patty's Family Restaurant. The coal tipple was located along the road. Truax recalled that mules carried the coal from the mine, and a large winch pulled it all up to Pennsylvania Avenue. At one time, near where Kosciuszko Hall is today, there was a large barn that was remodeled sometime between 1915 and 1920 and was used for country dances on Saturday nights.

Weirton Heights continued to grow, and by the late 1930s, it was incorporated as its own city, with James Stephenson elected its first mayor. The city building was built near the corner of Seventeenth Street and Pennsylvania Avenue on May 7, 1939. The flagpole is still standing on the lot today. The city of Weirton Heights was short-lived, as in 1947, the separate towns of Weirton Heights, Marland Heights and Holiday's Cove, in addition

Above: Weirton Heights City Building, built in 1939 and located on Pennsylvania Avenue near Seventeenth Street. *Weirton Area Museum and Cultural Center.*

Left: Photograph of Weirton founder E.T. Weir (*standing*) and Thomas Millsop (*seated*). *Weirton Area Museum and Cultural Center.*

to the unincorporated area of North Weirton, came together to form the current city of Weirton, with Tom Millsop, then president of Weirton Steel, as the first mayor.

Time marches on, and with every passing year, the stories of our neighborhoods change, too. To our predecessors, Weirton Heights was nothing more than a small farming community above the eighteenth-century village of Holliday's Cove, but to me, it's my home—and one that has a fascinating history.

Immigrants

When my wife and I moved back to Weirton after ten years away, we were blessed to be able to move into a home my parents own that has been in our family for generations. My great-grandfather Peter Zuros built the house back in the early 1950s. Since I have been spending time in this space, I have found myself reflecting on him and other immigrants like him who came to this country for a better life.

Peter was born in 1886 in Lithuania and immigrated to this country around 1911. First working in a copper mine, he eventually moved his family to the Ohio Valley, finally settling in Weirton. Before they came here, according to family tradition, my great-grandmother and some of their children died of the Spanish flu. Living through two world wars, struggling to move to a new country, learning a new language and somehow building a life in a new land is nothing short of heroic.

Most of us in this valley have ancestors like this. The mills of Weirton and Steubenville attracted many immigrants to our area. Weirton historically had more than fifty ethnic groups all coming here to work, and most of them are still represented here, as evidenced by the many ethnic organizations, clubs and churches that are still very active around here. A sizable community of immigrants settled in and around North Weirton along the lettered avenues. As time went on and the city of Weirton built up, those folks who settled in North Weirton moved up to the hills, away from the dirt and grime of the mills, to the more spacious neighborhoods of Weirton Heights, Marland Heights, Weircrest and others. Eventually, the mill would purchase much of the original townsite in North Weirton and demolish most of the buildings there. The streets are all still there, but the once-thriving immigrant community is gone.

One street I see every day in North Weirton is the block of Avenue A between Third and Fourth Streets. I have a panoramic photograph in my dining room of that block taken on July 7, 1934, on the occasion of the dedication of Weirton's Garibaldi Club. The Garibaldi Club, assembled in front of what was known as Columbia Hall, was in the middle of the block, flanked by two buildings: the one on the left was the Chios Grocery, and on the right was the Leader Market. Across Third Street from the Leader Market was Frank Kliers Garage, in which a large painted advertisement, "Chew Mail Pouch Tobacco," is visible in the photo. Behind the photographer would have been the All Saints Greek Orthodox Church. Around that area, on Avenue A, stood up to ten grocery stores and several coffeehouses, most of them ethnic in nature to serve a specific community. So many groups were represented there, such as Italians, Greeks and Serbians, among others. The Chios Grocery was a particularly long-lasting establishment, serving the community under the direction of the Karnoupakis brothers, Angelo and James, for forty-seven years. Natives of Chios, Greece, these immigrants arrived in America in 1916, started the store in 1921 and served the community of North Weirton at its location at 126 Avenue A for decades. Specialties of the store were imported cheeses, olives, honey and olive oil from Greece. According to the brothers, J.C. Williams, president of Weirton Steel between 1929 and 1936, was a frequent customer of the store,

Postcard view of Main Street and Avenue G in North Weirton. *Author's collection.*

This July 1934 photograph depicts the opening of the Weirton Garibaldi Lodge on Fourth Street in North Weirton. The Chios Grocery is visible in the background (above). *Author's collection.*

This July 1934 photograph depicts the opening of the Weirton Garibaldi Lodge on Fourth Street in North Weirton. The Chios Grocery is visible in the background (above). *Author's collection.*

where he would drink coffee and visit with steelworkers. Today, that block is completely empty, with nothing left but memories.

James, Angelo and Peter lived the American dream, established a home in a new land and were successful. James summed it up nicely in 1968, when the brothers sold the store: "We came to this country with a dream and we found it. Now that we depart from this building…we are proud."

ALL SAINTS IN THE NORTH END

I have always been fascinated by stories of Weirton's North End. I knew that the city started there, after all, in its earliest years by Weirton Steel as a settlement to provide the necessary manpower the mill would require. This was our version of the company town, like those one reads about in rural areas, although there was no company store or scrip. In Weirton, the company laid out streets, provided infrastructure and encouraged workers to own their own homes. A substantial investment was provided by the company to ensure that its workforce had a community to work and live in. With the expansion of the mills and the population, the North End became a bustling place full of shops, amenities, theaters, restaurants and the like, with the ever-present mill that made all of it possible looming just across Main Street from all of this new construction.

The North End was also the location of many of the immigrant communities that were established in the wake of the mill. Weirton Steel provided jobs to anyone willing to work, regardless of ethnic origin. Each immigrant group had its own gathering place that served as the center of the community, and for most of these groups, this place was their church.

In 1916, below Main Street on Avenue A across from the Chios Market and the Fourth Street intersection, a group of Greek immigrants laid the cornerstone of a new church that would be the All Saints Greek Orthodox Church. The Greek community raised $25,000 to build their house of worship in the new community and later added a parochial school in the rear of the property for their children. The Greek immigrants in the North End were many, and a multitude of establishments owned by Greek families sprang up around the church. A great publication that I turn to when looking at not just the Greek community in the North End but others, too, is a book called *Memoirs of North Weirton*, by John Pandelios. John was a wonderful man and someone I looked up to as a repository of Weirton's early history. John was born in 1916 on Avenue B in North Weirton and into his nineties could recall events and places with astonishing clarity. Working with Dennis Jones and the Weirton Museum, John put together this fascinating history of his old neighborhood. John also was a lifelong member of All Saints. It was always interesting to hear him talk about the various places he remembered in the old neighborhood.

As Weirton grew, so did the Greek community in town. By the 1940s, the old church building was showing its age, and the community needed a new place that would be able to accommodate the growing congregation. The current site of the church, on West Street, was selected, and the cornerstone was laid in 1947, ensuring that this community, started by dedicated Greek immigrants, would last into the future. Recently, I received as a gift a beautiful copy of the *2017 Centennial Album* of All Saints, and included in this was a DVD copy of a film depicting the building of the church in the late 1940s. What struck me while watching the film was that the congregation helped construct the building. Men, women and children assisted in its construction from the ground up, and watching these folks build the church was nothing short of inspiring. According to the centennial album, the name All Saints comes from the fact that each immigrant came from a different place in Greece that had its own unique patron saint. To honor all these patron saints, the name All Saints was chosen.

The new All Saints Greek Orthodox Church located on West Street. The building was built by the congregation and dedicated in 1950. *Weirton Area Museum and Cultural Center.*

The church today still maintains connections to its early beginnings in the North End. In the building, there are icons painted by one of the first pastors, Father Neophitos Iosafeos. He slept in the church as he completed the beautiful icons. The original church building, too, is actually still in existence in the North End. As the Greek community built the West Street edifice, the original building was moved in 1948 and was used for the St. Peters AME Church on County Road; the move was arranged by Sam Aria. John Pandelios recalled that the building was transported from its location on Avenue A up the street using a tractor trailer. Due to the steep incline, the building was dismantled in sections, then rebuilt in its current location.

The Greek community in Weirton has survived over one hundred years due to the dedication of the early immigrants who came to this country seeking a better life in America. They sought to establish a church for worship and to keep their customs and culture alive in this new land. Over the years, they have contributed greatly to our community and region, and there is no doubt, after looking at their history, that great things are yet to come.

ITALIAN IMMIGRANTS

America is a melting pot. It is a place where folks of all creeds, religions, ethnicities and backgrounds can come and make a better life for themselves and their families. I really like the term *melting pot*, especially for our area, because most of the ethnic groups came here to work in our steel industry, where the process of making steel involved melting raw ingredients together to form a finished product. Looking at the different folks who worked in our plants and factories, many were immigrants, or first-generation Americans who still had strong ties to their original homelands.

At the beginning of the twentieth century, millions of immigrants came to the New World from the Old. In the Old World, immigrants needed to travel to the nearest seaport to board the ship for their long journey to America. The ports that supplied the vast number of immigrants to the United States between the years 1900 and 1920 were Hamburg, Germany; Liverpool, England; Bremen, Germany; and Naples, Italy. In 1907 alone, the Italian port processed over 240,000 immigrants on their way to a new life in the United States. The reasons for immigration were many. Most folks were escaping poverty or military obligations or simply seeking to increase their opportunities for a better life.

Photograph of the Canzano family taken in Italy in 1915: Armando and Carmen (*first row*); Joseph, Maria and Gaetano *second row*); and Carmella, Antoinetta, Sophia and Mary (*third row*). *Cathy Adam.*

Upon arriving in the States, the immigrants either stayed in cities like New York or Philadelphia looking for work—or if they were lucky, they already had a destination in mind. Such was the case for many of the immigrants to our area. Weirton and Steubenville were certainly destinations for those looking for jobs. And as immigrants arrived, many sent letters back home to the Old World telling of the opportunities here.

Such was the case for my grandfather Joseph Delli Carpini's family. He was one of five children in his immediate family; two of them were born here in the States and the others in Gallo Matese, in the region of Campania, Italy. Like many immigrants, my great-grandfather was what was known as a bird of passage, traveling to the United States to work and collect funds to send back to his wife and children in Italy. Finally, in 1922, he had saved enough to bring his family to the United States. He was here already; my great-grandmother Antoinetta Canzano Delli Carpini, originally from Teano, Italy, along with her small children, made the perilous journey by boat to meet him. As far as I know, she never returned to Italy. But because the mills of Weirton provided good jobs, many residents from Gallo Matese ended up here. That, I am sure, was a comfort to her and many from that region: familiar names and faces in a strange land. The town of Reggio Calabria in southern Italy provided many immigrants to our area, as well.

When the immigrants arrived in our cities, they naturally chose to form communities based on their ethnicities. In Steubenville, the Italian area of town was the south end, consisting of South Fifth, Sixth and Seventh Streets, south of Adams Street. The community centered on the churches. St. Anthony, located on South Seventh Street, was founded in 1906, and the church building was completed and dedicated on April 3, 1910. According to a *Herald Star* article of the time, the cornerstone was laid with the inscription "Ecclesia Sancti, Antonii, Fundata, A.D. 1910" (the Church of Saint Anthony, founded in 1910). The church was built to support and minister to the many Italian American families in that neighborhood. It was here in this neighborhood that Dino Crocetti, better known as Dean Martin, was born in 1917, at 319 South Sixth Street. The Italian neighborhood thrived with Italian-owned stores and businesses in the first half of the twentieth century, but as time went by, the old Italian neighborhood declined as children and grandchildren of these Italian immigrants moved to the west end of Steubenville. In 2008, St. Anthony's closed after nearly one hundred years as an active parish.

The Italian neighborhood in Weirton was located in the North End around Third, Fourth, Fifth and Sixth Streets, in addition to Avenue A.

Passport photograph taken in July 1922 of Antoinetta Canzano, twenty-five, and her two children: Maria, four (*left*), and Tommy, two (*right*). They made the perilous journey across the Atlantic on board the *America*, arriving at Ellis Island in September 1922. *Thomas Carpini.*

This was where the first homes and businesses were erected in the area that would become the new community of Weirton. Looking at the Sanborn fire insurance maps of this area from 1915, one can see that the homes were exactly alike, typical of any company town. From the maps, one can see where the early residents lived and worked in the neighborhood. There were many barbers, two bakeries, several poolrooms, tailors and drugstores. A moving-picture house was located at the corner of Main Street and Avenue B. In 1923, between Avenue B and C on the mill side of Main Street, there were nine "bunk houses," presumably for mill workers, with a large, shared latrine in the rear of the buildings. This was on a street listed as "Greek." I have also seen it listed as "Chios Street." Many immigrants lived in this area.

For the Italian Americans in this neighborhood of Weirton, the center of life was family and community. The Garibaldi Hall on Avenue A was a focal point, as well as the Catholic church. As time went on, the Italian community prospered, and those who lived in the old neighborhood sought new homes away from the crowded area near the mill.

Between 1880 and 1924, over four million Italian immigrants came to the United States, and although they originally stayed in close-knit communities, they persevered and assimilated into American life. Coming full circle, in 2007, I visited Italy, and while visiting Naples, I took a trip to the island of Capri. We left from the port, and I thought of my great-grandmother Antoinetta and my great-aunts and uncles who left Italy from this very same port in 1922. As mainland Italy faded behind them, consisting of their past joys and struggles in addition to everything they ever knew, they had but one choice: to look to the future. I wish I could have asked them what they thought when they saw the Statue of Liberty in New York City. She welcomed them, saying, "Give me your tired, your poor, your huddled masses yearning to breathe free."

THE POLISH PARISH

Any visitor to my office will not be surprised to see many local objects and artifacts I have collected over the years. I love to collect locally from both sides of the river, and I am always keen to add more to my collection. I have others on the lookout for me, too, and it was from my parents that I received one of my most treasured local pieces. This object may not look like much, but to me it is special and holds so much local and personal family history. It consists of two plain bricks mounted on a marble base. The bricks have now taken on the role of bookends. One is plain, and the other has a gold plaque that reads, "A remembrance from a wonderful church—Old Sacred Heart of Mary 1919–1966." I think my mother picked these up at a rummage sale years ago and presented them to me, and I have treasured them ever since.

The building these two bricks came from was Sacred Heart of Mary Church, located in Weirton's North End on Avenue F. I certainly don't remember the building personally, but I have seen many pictures of both the interior and exterior. Growing up, I heard many stories of the church, always described as "Sacred Heart on Avenue F" to exclude it from the present church on Weirton Heights. My father's family were members of the parish, and many of their stories begin with Sacred Heart.

Speaking to visitors to our area, I often refer to Sacred Heart as the Polish church, especially when I talk of our history. The church has long been ethnically Polish, and that goes back to the very beginning of the parish. According to the West Virginia Encyclopedia, published by the West Virginia Humanities Council, Poles were the third-largest immigrant group in West Virginia in 1908, and when Weirton was settled in 1909, the Poles followed. As the population of Poles increased, a church was needed to minister to area Catholics. In 1910, Bishop P.J. Donahue of the Diocese of Wheeling sent the Reverend Father M. Madert, who spoke many languages—an important skill in an immigrant town. Father Madert was able to speak to most of the parishioners, especially the Poles, in their native language. In 1911, he oversaw construction of the first Catholic church in the Weirton area, St. Peter and Paul Parish, located on Avenue A on land donated by the mill. This building, according to the Sacred Heart of Mary's one hundred years memorial album, was built for $800 and could seat only one hundred persons. By 1915, the parish had outgrown the building, with many in the congregation coming from different ethnic backgrounds. Because of this, there was not much common ground among parishioners. So, the bishop divided the parish in two, one called St. Paul's, under Father Leo Monaco, and one called Saint Michael the Archangel, under Father M. Pawlowski. In 1916, Father Pawlowski was replaced by Father Andrew Wilczek, who

Postcard view of the intersection of County Road and Main Street in North Weirton. St. Paul's Church is seen at right. *Author's collection.*

served the parish for the remainder of his life. It was in that year that the name Sacred Heart of Mary was given to the parish.

Sacred Heart still remained at the original Avenue A location during World War I. At that time, many young Polish men who had recently immigrated to the United States heard the call from their native homeland and joined the conflict under General Józef Haller. This group of soldiers commanded by Haller was raised in the United States, trained in Canada, fought with the French on the western front during World War I and became the first free Polish army since the Polish legions who fought under Napoleon. Many of our local Polish immigrants joined the fight, including my great-grandfather Albin Kaminski. After the war, in 1920, the U.S. government brought back those who had enlisted in the United States, giving them the chance to become U.S. citizens based on their participation in the conflict. Albin took advantage of that opportunity in 1936. One of my cherished possessions is his army uniform from World War I and his flag of the Polish Falcons, which he carried to honor a free Poland after the war. General Haller did actually come to Weirton in 1934 and visited the church, much to the honor of local Polish veterans.

The people of Sacred Heart also gave much to the war effort in World War I by helping to raise $100,000 toward Poland's recovery after the war, a large sum even by today's standards. By 1919, a new building was needed to house the parish, and in September, the cornerstone was laid for the church on Avenue F. It was completed in 1920.

The church on Avenue F was the center of life for the Polish community for almost fifty years, celebrating baptisms, weddings, first communions and funerals. During World War II, the people of the parish held a mass for servicemen every Wednesday. From the parish, S. Arboczwski, A. Binkowski, W. Dziatkowicz, R. Gromek, H. Gwizdala, F. Haber, H. Kazienko, F. Klakos, A. Kost, H. Krukowski, S. Obrcmski, F. Pawlowski, F. Rakowski, T. Sagan, J. Sitarz, S. Szmagaj, F. Szymanek, W. Trojanowski, E. Zajac and T. Zgurki gave their lives for their country. Lest we forget their sacrifice.

In 1949, Father Emil Dobosz came to the parish as associate pastor, eventually becoming pastor in 1960 after the death of Father Wilczek. Father Dobosz oversaw the construction of the new church on Preston Avenue and the demolition of the old on Avenue F, moving the Blessed Sacrament to the new church on Weirton Heights in 1968.

Since the erection of the new church, Sacred Heart of Mary has remained the center of the Polish community in Weirton. The church has kept the traditions of the Polish Picnic and the annual Lenten Fish Fry alive, along with the incorporation of Polish customs in the parish. Any visitor to the

View of Sacred Heart of Mary Church on Avenue F. *Weirton Area Museum and Cultural Center.*

parish today will be met with a beautiful sanctuary, described by my wife as jewel box, with an impressive stained-glass window behind the main altar, with one side describing the history of Poland and the other describing the history of Poles in America. The parish also has many elements of the original church on Avenue F incorporated into its worship space. It is a beautiful and sacred space that transcends the history of the Polish Catholic community in our town. Today, the parish is under the direction of its pastor, Father Dennis Schuelkens, and its associate pastor, Father Tony Thurston, two priests who inspire their congregations every day to live out Christ's call in our lives. I pray that the tradition and legacy of the parish will last long in the future, as it has for the last 111 years.

VETERANS' STORIES

Veterans Day is a time to remember and honor all those who have served in our military. Those who have said yes to service and have given of their time and energy to protect our country deserve our heartfelt thanks. Truly, it is due to their sacrifices that we have the nation we live in today. My maternal grandfather, Joseph D. Carpini, served as a military policeman in England, France, Belgium and finally, in April 1945, Germany. My paternal grandfather, Paul M. Zuros, was first sent to the Aleutian Islands to prepare for a possible Japanese invasion of Alaska in the early years of World War II. He was later sent to Europe, serving in France, Belgium, Germany and Austria by the end. Both men traveled extensively during the war years, and both gave their early twenties to the army. It is this sacrifice and those of countless others that we often take for granted. On Veterans Day, when I look into the faces of my children, I remember that so many gave so much for this life we live. "Thank you" somehow falls short.

My grandfathers both came from Weirton and experienced the rise and later boom of the steel industry. So much was built and enlarged at Weirton Steel in anticipation of the Second World War. Expansion and enlargement of the capacities of furnaces and output was the order of the day. When I witness the dismantlement of the mills and factories of the former Weirton Steel Company, it is with mixed emotions. I know that the era of history that enabled companies like Weirton Steel to boom are over. The time to look to the future is here. It was in that same vein that when the basic oxygen plant (BOP), or "Mill of the Future," was built in the mid-1960s, another building, tied to much history and memories, was demolished to make way for the future.

Along Main Street in Weirton, close to the main office, a group of warehouses was transformed in the 1940s to produce the eight-inch howitzer shell, one of the very few completed products ever made at Weirton Steel during the war. This was an incredible operation, from casting the steel for the projectiles, to engineering and building the machines to make the shells, to sending the completed shell casings on their way to the front lines. Weirton Steel engineered the total process. The mill workers at that time were local high school students, critical war workers and women. Many people came from the community to work in the mills during the war. Plants like Weirton Steel were doing their part to win the war for the Allies.

Surely, my grandfathers both encountered steel made by Weirton Steel in the army overseas. Along with the shells from the plant, steel components

Joseph Carpini while he was serving as a military policeman in Europe during World War II. *Author's collection.*

for tanks, trucks and ships were made by Weirton Steel. Products made from brass, copper, silver chloride and magnesium and .30- to .50-caliber ammunition were also made at the mill. Most importantly, over 5,000 men from Weirton Steel's workforce went to fight during the war. Over 115 gave the supreme sacrifice to our country.

The days of the booming mill are over. The skies are clear, when they were once full of smoke. While on Veterans Day, we honor those who serve, I also want to say thank you in a small way to the mill workers who "fought the battle of production" to supply all the servicemen and women overseas who fought for our freedoms. They made the supplies and equipment necessary to keep our servicemen safe, and that's not a small thing. As we close that chapter in our history, we welcome new opportunities for growth to our region. And just as the mills filled the land of the Ohio Valley, we hope new things will fill their place, too. Even as those old behemoths are torn down, the history of what the company did for our families, our nation

A group of soldiers inspect female workers in Weirton Steel's howitzer shell plant during World War II. *Weirton Area Museum and Cultural Center.*

and our veterans will live on in the freedoms we all share. Let us never take for granted the sacrifices of our veterans or those who support them here at home. "Thank you" is not enough.

WEIRTON SPORTS

On a Friday evening recently, my family and I decided to attend a Weir High football game. It had to be my first Friday night high school football game for at least fifteen years or more. In fact, the last time I was at a game was down at the old Jimmy Carey Stadium in downtown Weirton, off Virginia Avenue. Nestled between a hillside and the mill, the complex was full of character. The old concrete stands were unique, and I have a distinct memory of spectators, mostly older men, standing under the announcer's booth smoking cigars and cigarettes while watching the game. The white smoke rising, mixing with the cool autumn air underneath those giant floodlights, made the scene memorable. And who could forget the announcing of Bob Rossell, whose distinct voice would echo in the night, bouncing off the smokestacks and walls of the nearby sheet mill amid the cheering crowd.

I always thought the old stadium was a bit out of place, to be fair. It seemed that it was tucked away and not very accessible to the visiting team. My family would often park downtown on Main Street near the Strip Steel office and walk up to the stadium. We would sometimes stop at an establishment called "The 48." My father tells me that at one time, the hot mill in Weirton Steel could roll a forty-eight-inch slab of steel into a coil (hence the name) weighing around twenty tons on average, depending on the length and customer specifications. (Later, the hot mill expanded its capacity to roll a fifty-four-inch slab.) The 48 was near mill gate 5—you could see it from the front door—and it was a popular spot for mill workers and families before the Weir High game. In that place, mill workers could cash their paychecks, but the cashier would keep any change as a payment for the service. The business had been there a long while, since before the 1950s—certainly before my time—and I remember it being packed before the games. Moving out of The 48 with my friends, we would start the climb up Virginia Avenue to the stadium. On the corner of Virginia Avenue and West Street, there once stood the old Beth Israel Jewish Synagogue; one morning, before a Weir High game, it fell down. The building had been built in 1927 and was obviously in a state of disrepair. We would pass the telephone building, now the Union Hall, and move past the packed parking lots of the mill to the stadium.

The stadium was not always by itself; it was once part of the complex of the old Weir high school that faced Orchard Street. Those buildings—built in 1917 and 1923, respectively—ceased to be a high school in 1963 and were demolished in the early 1980s. Since around 1794, the location of the old Weir High stadium was occupied by the Griffith House. This stone building served as a blockhouse during a time in our local history when the threat of Native American attacks was common in our area. If threatened with attack, nearby settlers could move to this fortified stone building to fend off their enemy. The Griffith House was demolished to make way for the new stadium, which, according to local historian Dennis Jones in his book *Weirton: A Pageant of Nations*, "was completed during the summer of 1935 at a

Scene from a night game at Weir High's Jimmy Carey Stadium in downtown Weirton. *Weirton Area Museum and Cultural Center.*

cost of $50,000, and on Labor Day, the Second Annual Festival of Nations would become the first official event to take place there attracting more than 15,000 visitors." The Festival of Nations was an idea, according to Jones, that was put forth in Weir High's 1929 yearbook, where all of Weirton's nationalities were represented in a pageant. The first festival, in 1934, was held at the new Margaret Manson Weir Memorial Pool on Marland Heights, where, according to Jones, an estimated ten thousand people gathered for the festivities. The festival was "designed to be noncompetitive and create a sense of fellowship and unity among the various ethnic groups and also provide comforting memories of their homeland." From 1935 through 1944, the event was held at the stadium annually, although during the Second World War, the festival turned from celebrating distinct nationalities to promoting our common effort in those days, the cause of freedom, and inspiring patriotism at that trying time.

After the festivals ended, the stadium was just home to high school football. The first football game to be held at the stadium occurred on September 21, 1935; Weir defeated Cleveland South 14–0. Also in that year, Coach Carl

Weir High School on Orchard Street, covered with ivy. *Weirton Area Museum and Cultural Center.*

Hamill led the team to a season record of 10–0–0, and the school was state champ. The first night game occurred on September 16, 1938; Weir defeated Follansbee 27–0. In 1981, the stadium was renamed Jimmy Carey Stadium after the late coach Jimmy Carey. Many students played at the stadium who later went on to professional careers. The Weirton Museum and Cultural Center maintains a list of professional athletes from Weirton—not just football players but also basketball and baseball players and professional golfers who have had a connection to Weirton at one time. This is not a complete list, but those who played on the field include Bob Gain, a Weir grad of 1947, who went on to play for the Ottawa Rough Riders and the Cleveland Browns; Bob Jeter, Weir grad of 1956, who went on to play for the Green Bay Packers and the Chicago Bears; Bill Tucker, Weir grad of 1962, who went on to play for the San Francisco 49ers and the Chicago Bears; Tony Jeter, Weir High grad of 1962, who went on to play for the Pittsburgh Steelers; Gene Trosch, a Madonna grad of 1963, who went on to play for the Kansas City Chiefs; and in my day, Quincy Wilson, a Weir High grad of 1999, who went on to play for the Atlanta Falcons and Cincinnati Bengals. The list goes on, and it is very impressive that so many professionals came from our city and excelled in sports. Today, there is a marker, made from the goalpost from the old Weir High stadium at the corner of Cove Road and Weir Avenue, that lists known athletes from Weirton. The marker was installed in 2014. It is appropriate that it is located along Weir Avenue, as that street has the distinction of having produced at least seven professional athletes, all within a few blocks. Weirton's sports heritage is rich.

The history of the old stadium came to a close on October 28, 2011, when Weir High played its last game on the field against East Liverpool, losing 40–0. After seventy-six years of community events, the gates were closed for the last time to the cheering fans, enthusiastic bands and determined players. The following August, the new Jimmy Carey Stadium was dedicated, next to Weir High. This place now holds about a decade of memories for a new generation of students and members of our community. I am sure that if the new place lasts as long as the old stadium, great things are bound to happen on that field.

HISTORY IS A SPLASH

With high temperatures and sunny days so typical of Ohio Valley summers, one is compelled to think of ways to cool off. In the past, if you didn't have access to a clean spring or creek nearby, the best thing to do was visit your local pool. For most of us growing up in the Weirton area, we had the choice of a few local pools, depending on where you lived or, most importantly, where your friends went. And some of us lucky devils even worked at these great recreation facilities. In high school, I was a lifeguard for a few summers. The best part about working at the pool in those days was getting paid to sit in the sun with a cold drink in my hand for hours on end. I always went by the mantra, "A good lifeguard never gets wet." Only once did I have to help someone get out of the pool in the years I worked. Perhaps the poolgoers did not appreciate the strict rules I tried to enforce, but on the other hand, no one got hurt, either.

The pool I spent the most time at in my youth was Lynnwood Park Swim Club, located on Lisa Court off Culler Road in Pleasant Valley. Although a membership was required to swim, there were always many families who took advantage of the amenities. The pool was located next to the old number 9 hole—later the eighteenth—of the Pleasant Valley golf course, and often, golfers would tee off then swing by the fence for a cold drink or to talk to poolgoers. Sitting by the pool on a chaise lounge overlooking the golf course was always relaxing. Lynnwood was constructed by the Sellitti family in 1964 and is still privately owned today. According to an article in the *Weirton Daily Times* in October that year, "The recreation center offers a main pool measuring 75 by 50 and a kiddie pool 25 by 25, both featuring overhead and underwater lights for night swimming. The swim club offers a heated pool to insure comfortable swimming from early May until late September." Lifeguards that first season were Stephanie Gordon, William Ludewig and Daniel Allen, with Michael Rumora as pool manager. My mother, Jolene, was a lifeguard there as well, some years after it opened. The pool today still looks as beautiful and relaxing as I am sure it did in the 1960s. For me, summer simply isn't summer without Lynnwood.

On Weirton Heights, families could also go to Starvaggi Pool, part of Starvaggi Memorial Park, given, as the paper described it in May 1968, "as a gift to the residents of Weirton by Starvaggi Charities, Inc., through the generosity of Mr. and Mrs. Michael Starvaggi, one of Weirton's foremost philanthropic families." The pool was part of a forty-five-acre complex that still hosts picnic and recreation facilities. The pool itself was composed of sixteen acres and at the time of its dedication was considered "the finest outdoor swimming pool in West Virginia measuring 165 feet long and 55 feet wide." Included also was a "baby pool, a spacious parking lot, the most modern filtering plant available and a large building that housed offices, showers and locker rooms and concession stand." The building at that time had a flat roof that also served as additional seating, especially during busy days. And there was many a day in the summer that if you didn't get to the pool early, there was no space on the benches or on the stands to lay your towel. On hand at the dedication was the Weir High Band, Mr. and Mrs. Starvaggi, J.G. Redline, Mrs. Tom Millsop and Mayor Frank Rybka, among others, with Don Donell serving as MC. Mr. Anthony Torchio, Weirton recreation director, explained

July 1968 photograph of Starvaggi Pool, a gift to the City of Weirton by the Starvaggi family. *Weirton Area Museum and Cultural Center.*

the admission rates: "The fee for Weirton residents will be 50 cents for adults and 25 cents for children and students, while season passes would be $15 per family; $10 each adult; $7 student." What I remember most about the pool was the deep end, measuring thirteen feet at its deepest, with several diving boards serving the space. Now diving boards at Starvaggi pool are a thing of the past, but with the addition of the splash pad area and the water slides, there is still a lot of fun to be had at the pool.

The longest-serving pool in Weirton by far was the Margaret Manson Weir Memorial Pool in Marland Heights Park. Given as a gift by E.T. Weir and the estate of his late brother David in honor of their mother, the pool opened in 1934 and served the community of Weirton for seventy-one years, with Carl Hamill serving as director from the day it opened through the 1967 season. Arguably the most architecturally and aesthetically pleasing of the three Weirton pools, the unique complex was designed by the Bintz Swimming Pool Company and added to the National Register of Historic Places in 1993. As of 2018, there were only 19 Bintz pools still standing out of possibly 120 ever built, with only 8 in operation serving their intended purpose. The pool

The Margaret Manson Weir Memorial Pool, named in honor of E.T. Weir's mother and built with funds from the estate of the late David Weir, E.T. Weir's brother. The pool and park opened on July 4, 1934. *Weirton Area Museum and Cultural Center.*

is aboveground and ovoid in shape, which makes it pretty unique as pools go. Books could be written about the memories folks have of this pool. From summers spent at the pool, to high dives, to dances, picnics, orchestras and graduation parties in the park, this Weirton landmark has been present through it all. For most folks who lived in other parts of the city, a trip to the pool almost always included walking the path at the end of Brookline Drive from downtown up through the woods to the park. This shortcut really was to save bus fare up Marland Heights Road and to dry off on the return journey. For almost fifty years, the pool was under the management of Weirton Steel, and in 1983, the pool was turned over to the City of Weirton. In 2005, the pool closed its doors to the public after its long career of serving the needs of our community, especially on hot summer days.

Although many of us today are blessed with backyard pools at our own homes, nothing seems to replace the memories made with friends at the public pools in our community. Take a trip down memory lane by visiting these special places soon. Pull up a lounge, get a drink and relax the summer days away.

WEIRTON'S LOST TREASURE

Most small children are excited by buried treasure, and my son Paulie is no exception. There is something exciting about hearing a story, finding a treasure map and following it to "X marks the spot." The appeal is the adventure of the hunt and the hope of discovering something lost. For my son, anyway, adventure, pirates, sailing ships and treasure seem to hold his interest at this moment. The other night, when he asked me if there was any buried treasure near us, I had to say no—at least in the sense of pirate treasure, anyway. After all, we are a long way from the ocean. After some thought, I was reminded of a case of reported buried loot—not gold doubloons, but cash—reportedly buried someplace in our region.

On Wednesday, November 10, 1920, the Farmers Deposit National Bank in downtown Pittsburgh carefully prepared the payroll of the Weirton Steel Company to be sent in two packages to the Bank of Weirton by registered mail. The packages, containing a total of $93,000 between them, left the bank after being sealed in canvas sacks and tagged for registered mail. A bank messenger delivered the bags from the bank to the Pittsburgh Post Office, and they were subsequently locked up. That evening, the mail was sent to Pittsburgh's Union Station for transit the next morning on the first train to Weirton. After the mail arrived in Weirton, it was transported a half mile from Weirton's Pennsylvania station to the post office and then on to the Bank of Weirton, where it was discovered that the $93,000, in denominations of twenties, tens, fives and ones, was missing. In its place was stacks of currency-sized clippings from Pittsburgh newspapers dated Thursday, November 11, 1920.

Immediately, the crime was reported to the post office, the insurance company that insured the shipment and the local authorities. A full-on federal investigation began quietly. News of the heist broke to the press the following Monday. The story made national headlines, appearing in papers as far away as Alaska. Fortunately, there was no interruption in workers' paychecks, as the necessary cash was brought instead from Steubenville banks on short notice. As luck would have it, the money had been insured before it left the bank.

In the weeks and months following the heist, the investigation continued. Rumors stated that there were suspects, but no arrests were made. Theories abounded about the manner in which the money was stolen. One theory suggested that the money was thrown from the train between Pittsburgh and Weirton, but interviews between Department of Justice agents and the crew of the train proved to be fruitless. In April 1922, authorities discovered $17,000, but it could not be confirmed that it was part of the loot. News of the investigation fell largely silent until October 1923, when an article in the *Steubenville Herald-Star* suggested a possible lead. Three Weirton men had been tracked down in connection with the robbery. Federal agents had been working for years infiltrating the community to find leads, one even going so far as to pose as a fruit salesman to learn information. It was reported that the prime suspect was the driver of the mail truck between the Weirton train station and the post office. The biggest piece of evidence was the fact that when the canvas mailbags were given to the driver in Weirton, they were reportedly clean, new bags, but officials at the Bank of Weirton were given old, soiled bags. And since the cut-up newspapers were dated Thursday, officials decided that the heist happened after the train left Pittsburgh early that morning. Also around that time, a sum of $9,000 was found and traced back to the suspects, supposedly from the heist. The money smelled "musty," as if it had been hidden away in a damp place for a long time, and the federal agent posing as a fruit salesman was told that the bulk of the money was still hidden in Weirton. Indictments were made, and the suspects, who knew they were being followed, were tracked all over the country as well as internationally, but no arrests were made. In 1926, an article in the *East Liverpool Review-Tribune* mentioned that information was being sought regarding buried cash connected to a person who was

Early photograph of Avenue F and Second Street, later Main Street, in North Weirton. *Author's collection.*

wanted in the 1921 robbery of a bank in Imperial, Pennsylvania. Officials believed this person was also involved in the 1920 Weirton payroll robbery. It is general knowledge, the paper reported, that over $100,000 was buried in and around the Weirton–Steubenville area in a milk can.

The sum of $100,000 in 1926 would be the equivalent to around $1,450,000 in today's money. This is a huge sum of cash lost and possibly buried in our region. Could it still be out there? Sorry, Paulie; there is no map with an "X marks the spot" to solve this one-hundred-year-old mystery, but after all, there is some treasure in the thrill of the hunt!

GOING TO THE MOVIES

Recently, my son was invited to a birthday party at the Plaza Theater in Weirton. He had a wonderful time hanging out with his friends and enjoying popcorn and a drink while watching a movie on the big screen. He has attended a few parties there, and I appreciate that the theater offers these events for us in our community. His school has taken a few field trips to the place as a special treat for the students, as well.

When I was growing up, the Plaza was the place to be. It often had a new movie on Friday, which was shown at seven and again at nine o'clock. I was always excited to drive past the marquee on Penco Road to see what the next movie would be. When you arrived at the theater, the staff would charge admission and issue you a small square ticket that they ripped in half, keeping the stub. I'll never forget the smell of popcorn in that place. It has been years, but I still can smell it. Some things you don't forget. I think the first movie I ever saw in a theater was there, about 1991 or 1992. Truly, the Plaza Theater has a special place in our local history.

Going to the movie theater back in the day was a special event, and here in our area, you had many to choose from. In Weirton alone, there were up to nine theaters operating in our city over the years, based on the list compiled by local historian Dennis Jones. Even in Weirton's earliest days, there was a theater here, the first being the Weirton Theater at 266 Avenue B. The building shared a lot with a bakery in the rear of the property. It didn't last long, because by 1919, that theater was gone, replaced by a pool hall and a restaurant. A new theater showed up at 208 Avenue A; according to John Pandelios in his book *Memoirs of North Weirton*, that theater was known as the Olympic and later became the Colonial. This theater was owned by Charles Miller and Mike Stamatoulakis.

This 1971 photograph shows a busy Main Street near the Weirton Bus Terminal and Manuel's Dry Cleaners. *Weirton Area Museum and Cultural Center.*

At 333 Main Street there was another movie establishment called the Rex Theater, owned by the proprietors of the Colonial in addition to Gus Vallas. According to Pandelios, this establishment was right next to one of Weirton's earliest bowling places, called the Hayes Bowling Alley. The Rex shared space with the Vasilios Sofocleos Barber Shop, and on the second floor was the home of the Order of AHEPA (the American Hellenic Educational Progressive Association). Also on that block was the Mike Psaros Barber Shop, the Olympic Confectionary and the Frankovich and Sons Grocery Store.

On Main Street between E and F there were two theaters, the Manas and the State. These establishments were separated by an alley that went straight up to Weirton Elementary on County Road. The Manas was built by William Anas and was regarded as the main theater in town. The State was built by the Rabinovich family, and according to Pandelios, this place was known as the Ranch House because it showed only Westerns, especially on Saturday mornings. John also recounted that on the stage of the State, there was a wrestling match between two world-renowned professional wrestlers of the 1930s, Greek-born Jim Londos and Polish-born Stanislaus Zebisko. On that same block was a laundry, a barbershop, the Hub Men's Store, Gus Caravas Variety Store, Bears Department Store and Barr's Drugs. Later on, the Anas Theater opened on that same block at 1518 Main Street. According to Dennis Jones, all the theaters eventually were owned by the same company, Weir-Cove Enterprises, under Nick Anas.

The Strand Theater was located at 3216 Main Street, just inside the city of Holliday's Cove, which started in the middle of Ferguson Avenue. The Strand was located directly across Main Street from Greco-Hertnick Funeral Home. The manager in the 1930s was George Sturgeon. The other theater in downtown Weirton was the Cove Theater, located at 3405 Main Street, which is now the only theater building still standing downtown. It is located directly across Main Street from the Cove Presbyterian Church. According to Jones, the theater was originally called the Lincoln Theater, but its name was changed to the Cove before the 1940s. At Christmastime in the early 1940s, the Weirton Independent Union hosted free children's Christmas parties at the theater as a gift to the community. There are many pictures showing eager children watching the show. By 1964, the Cove had closed and become the Weirton Market.

According to Jones, the Belle-Aire Drive-In was founded in 1949 by Joseph Yacos on Weirton Heights in what is the Belle-Aire addition today. I remember seeing as a kid the old sign on Pennsylvania Avenue that looked like it had stepped out of the 1950s. My mother, Jolene, remembers visiting the drive-in: "My friends lived by the drive-in, we would go in through the gate and told the gate attendant we just wanted to go to the concession stand then watch part of the movie while sitting on the long bench in front of the concession stand/projection booth." This theater was also owned later by Weir-Cove Enterprises.

In October 1969, construction began on Weirton's Plaza Theater. According to the *Weirton Daily Times*, the theater was estimated to cost around $125,000 and featured seating for 336 people. On hand for the groundbreaking were John Gardner, owner of Gardner Theaters, which would own and operate the facility; Mike Starvaggi, president of the Weirton Shopping Plaza; Sam Schiappa of the F&S Construction Company; and Al Bundy of Starvaggi Enterprises. The Plaza was completed at the end of February 1970, and for the past fifty years, give or take a few, the Plaza has been in operation.

A 1941 view of the Anas Theater located at 1518 Main Street. *Weirton Area Museum and Cultural Center.*

The Plaza is a survivor in a world of streaming and on-demand movies. One can simply ask their smart TV to play a specific movie, and presto, there it is. One may argue that watching a movie at home is more comfortable, but it is just not the same as visiting a good old-fashioned movie theater. Maybe you will find some time soon to see a matinee or feature presentation. Make sure to get a bag of popcorn and make some new memories, too.

THE CENTER

One of the great perks of working in downtown Steubenville is that just near Historic Fort Steuben is the Antiques Warehouse located in the old Demarks Building. Here, one can spend a lot of time perusing three floors of treasures. When I worked at the fort, whenever I had a few minutes and the weather was nice, I popped on over and visited my favorite booths. I am always on the lookout for a new object to add to my collection, and inevitably, I would stumble upon something—a piece of furniture, for example—that I'd consider buying. Despite my father's words ringing in my head that the best collectibles are those one can carry home in one's pocket, I do sometimes fall for the allure of the antique.

On a recent visit to the Antiques Warehouse, I was delighted to find a little souvenir booklet from the dedication of the Weirton Community Center. As it turns out, the center was dedicated in March 1952, exactly seventy years ago at the time of this writing. As a historian, I couldn't let the center's anniversary go by without writing about the great accomplishment of the city fathers, citizens and employees of Weirton Steel who made this building possible. Without their investment in our community so long ago, we may not have had this facility as the center of our community for the past seventy years.

The story of the center actually began in 1948, as was explained in the February edition of the *Weirton Steel Employees Bulletin*: "For many, many years, the people of Weirton have seen the need of a centrally located community institution to provide healthful recreation for children and adults and around which the cultural life of the city could revolve. The proposed new Weirton Community Center will be such a place, the fulfillment of a civic dream." And a dream it was. The new city of Weirton at that time was less than a year old. The city had been incorporated in April, and its first mayor, Thomas Millsop, was elected on June 1, 1947. Millsop had a very interesting history in his own right, working his way up through Weirton Steel management, and by this time in 1947 he had been president of Weirton Steel since 1936. Millsop would serve two terms as mayor of Weirton, and under his leadership, much was accomplished. Most notable was the construction of the Weirton General Hospital and the community center.

The estimated cost for the center, as explained by the bulletin in 1948, was more than $1,000,000. The organization that was set up to raise the funds was first the Community Service Council, then the Community Center Association, with Ray M. Corll serving as president. When the fundraising

A 1973 photograph of the Millsop Community Center. *Weirton Area Museum and Cultural Center.*

campaigned kicked off in February 1948, hopes were high that the people of the community would answer the call to donate. Weirton Steel generously donated $500,000 to the project, Thomas Millsop personally donated $25,000 and E.T. Weir, founder of Weirton Steel, donated $50,000. The employees of Weirton Steel, on the urging of the Weirton Independent Union and the Community Service Council/Community Center Association, set up a plan in which employees could donate one day's wages over five pay periods over three years to the project. This works out to a full week's pay for each employee toward the endeavor. Incredibly, in just seventeen days, the full amount of the building was pledged. According to David Javersak in his book *History of Weirton*, fifteen thousand contributors donated to the fund, with the citizens of Weirton donating around $650,000 of the total cost.

In 1950, final plans were drawn up by Steubenville architect John J. Rietz. His design is solidly what architectural historians would call now mid-century modern. And the drawings submitted by Rietz are generally what we see today in the building. The building originally was designed to encompass sixty-eight thousand square feet of floor space. The "hotel like" lobby would feature terrazzo floors, wood paneling and a large mural painted by Pittsburgh artist Edwin P. Couse. Ground was broken in 1950, with the Wheeling firm of Engstrom and Wynn taking on the construction.

Finally, in February 1952, the center was completed, and dedication ceremonies took place on March 1 and 2, 1952. The final cost amounted to $1,250,000; that's around $13,500,000 in today's dollars. The dedication of the building was elaborate, with officials turning over the building to the mayor and the City of Weirton. The dedication address was given by none other than E.T. Weir, followed by a performance by the Weirton Steel Male Chorus. The following day, the Wheeling Symphony Orchestra gave a concert. On March 4, Eleanor Steber of the Metropolitan Opera performed onstage.

What greeted the estimated 35,000 visitors over those few days was exciting. Most notable was the seventy-five-by-thirty-five-foot swimming pool holding 121,000 gallons of water that was recycled every eight hours. Above the pool, over 150 spectators could watch the aquatic activities. Dressing rooms near the pool were modern, and hair dryers were provided in the women's dressing rooms. The youth center was a popular spot with its own entrance. This center featured a large room for events, such as dances, that were held for youth. The snack bar was a popular spot in the youth center in those days. The Weirton Library was located in the building operated by the Weirton Women's Club. Twelve thousand or so books were moved to the new facility by the Boy Scouts, the Key Club and the Blue Jean Council. The gym was state-of-the-art and could hold over 2,000 people for an event or 1,600 for a basketball game. The stage in the gym was designed to accommodate larger productions due to a removable wall in the rear of the stage. During that first March, Tex Beneke and the Glenn Miller Orchestra performed on stage, in addition to the Weir High Band and the University of Michigan Symphony Band. A dining hall, capable of handling community events, came accompanied by a large kitchen for the preparation of meals. Other attractions included meeting rooms, anterooms and craft and exercise rooms, in addition to handball courts and a youth gym for kids under twelve. A sponsor's room was also included as a lounge area for men who gave more than fifty dollars a year to the center.

Over the years, the center has remained a focal point of our community. In 1965, the center was renamed for our first mayor, Thomas Millsop. At the dedication of the building in 1952, Millsop said, "The new Community Center is a product stamped: 'Made of Weirton Teamwork.'" It was provided by the people for the people and how much good derives from it depends in the final analysis on the people." I think the longevity of the building and the important services that are contained therein is a testament to its irreplaceable value in our community. Even after seventy years, the next generation of Weirton citizens continues to benefit from that investment.

THINGS THAT ARE GONE

Anyone who is from the tristate area who is interested in local history has seen, or at least is aware of, Rick Sebak's work on WQED Pittsburgh. His down-to-earth demeanor and documentary style of television program is addictive and draws the audience into whatever story he is telling. Typically, Sebak focuses on the Pittsburgh area in his programs, but he is such a dynamic storyteller that it is hard not to connect with the history. I feel that our area is so close to the Golden Triangle that their history is relevant to ours, too. Take, for instance, my seven-year-old son, who, despite never having being there, is absolutely enamored by Sebak's 1988 program *Kennywood Memories* and watches it often. Many evenings have been spent around the dinner table talking with him about the great rides, picnic memories and warm and carefree summer days spent there. Hopefully, soon, we can fulfill his wish to go to Kennywood so he can have Kennywood memories of his own.

In my estimation, Rick has succeeded in the job of a public historian. To preserve and promote history while inspiring a younger generation is ever the goal. I hope that with this book, I do a small part toward that end. For me, a few of the most interesting programs Rick produced were *Things That Aren't There Anymore* in 1990 and *Stuff That's Gone* in 1994. With that in mind, it's fun to take a look at our area and talk about a few places that are gone.

In Weirton, I would wager that one of the most dramatic changes to our landscape in the past few years is the ongoing demolition of Weirton Steel, most particularly the basic oxygen plant (BOP) or the "Mill of the Future," as it was known. The enormous building, completed in 1967, was a towering structure that dwarfed everything around it save the ancient hills between which it nestled in our valley. With the construction of the building and complex, buildings, homes and other plants—especially the shell plant so vital to arms production in World War II—were demolished to make way. The site is now vacant, awaiting the next chapter in our town's history. Returning to Weirton after the building was demolished took some getting used to.

Another significant change in our community landscape was the demolition of our city's public elementary schools. The list of schools demolished includes Cove School, which was built in 1912, closed in 1991 and is now the site of the Weirton Events Center; Weirton Grade School in the North End on County Road, built in 1913 and closed in 1963; Weirton Heights Elementary, built in 1925 on the corner of South Twelfth and School Streets and closed in 2014; Broadview Elementary, opened in

Postcard view of the Weirton Grade School located on County Road opposite Sacred Heart of Mary Church. *Author's collection.*

Aerial postcard view of the new Weir High School located on Weirton Heights. *Author's collection.*

1955 and closed in 2014; and Liberty Elementary School, built in 1939 and closed in 2014. I am personally attached to Liberty School, as that is the elementary school I attended growing up. I remember fondly the long, rambling hallways, the library and the distinctive 1930s green, beige and maroon color scheme of the floor and walls. If you looked closely at the masonry on the front of the building, you could see images and words pressed into these unique bricks. Dunbar School on Weir Avenue, built at the same time as Liberty, also has these distinctive brick motifs. Dunbar School, historic in its own right as a school for African Americans constructed before desegregation in 1955, is still in existence; it closed as a school in 1991 and is now privately owned. The other elementary schools in our city, Edgewood, Marland Heights Elementary and the L.B. Millsop School, are still standing.

One school building that is gone and that meant a great deal to many was the old Weir High School on Orchard Street downtown, built around 1923 to replace the old central school next door that had been built in 1916. The new building was described by Frank Pietranton in his 1936 book *History of Weirton and Holliday's Cove*: "This is a fireproof structure; large airy classrooms are provided for the students; a large gymnasium and an auditorium were included in the building. Laboratories for the science classes are fully equipped. Nothing is lacking which will help the young men and women of Weirton and Holliday's Cove to obtain an excellent high school education." The building later would be covered in ivy, which is one of the things remembered most about the place.

In January 1964, after the old Weir High School had been in use for many decades, four hundred students and faculty moved to the new campus-style Weir High School located on Weirton Heights.

The old Weir High School is gone now, demolished, and the stadium next door is overgrown. But still, we are connected to these things that are past. The places that hold our memories are not made of brick and mortar or even steel; they are the stories and memories we share with others. The new places in town, although not the same as those we knew, will be held dear to coming generations, and that is okay. It is the nature of things to change. Like Rick Sebak, who inspired my son to love Kennywood, we hopefully can inspire a new generation to see just what is so special about our little valley, and they can make their own memories to last a lifetime.

Chapter 5

BOTH SIDES OF THE RIVER

Presidential Visits

The decision on who to vote for as president is one that should not be taken lightly. The beauty of our system of government is that "we the people" have the power and responsibility to grant that office to the person who will best represent the interest of the people. Let your voice be heard in November, no matter whom you vote for. In the Ohio Valley, largely due to our industrial past, candidates for the presidency have visited us, hoping to win voters.

The very first president who visited our area was, in fact, our first. In October 1770, George Washington traveled down the Ohio River, stopping in Mingo Town. Washington may have been the president most personally familiar with our area, since he fought for control of the river during the French and Indian War. It's possible that other presidents used the river, but it wasn't until almost one hundred years later that another president came to town using a new mode of transportation.

On February 11, 1861, president-elect Abraham Lincoln left Springfield, Illinois, by train on his way to Washington for his inauguration. On February 14, he stopped in Cadiz Junction and, finally, made his way through Steubenville. Lincoln's train stopped for twenty minutes at the station platform located at the corner of Market and Water Streets. While his family stayed on the train, Lincoln greeted a large crowd of people. He gave a short speech on the rights explained in the Constitution and majority rule. At the signal of the train whistle, Lincoln boarded and started again toward Washington.

Very near the location of Lincoln's speech, an establishment named the Hotel Lacy, west of Market and High Streets, was said to have hosted President Grant. Built in 1798, this building, also known as the United States Hotel, served as the city hospital, the precursor to the Ohio Valley Hospital. Grant is said to have given a speech from the balcony that wrapped around the building, although there is no confirmed record of his visit. President Woodrow Wilson, on the other hand, had strong ties to the area, although we don't know if he ever visited. Wilson's grandfather James Wilson was the owner and editor of the *Herald Star* beginning in 1815. His parents, Joseph Wilson and Janet Woodrow, met in Steubenville while Janet was a student at the Steubenville Female Seminary. The family eventually moved south, but young Woodrow certainly must have been raised on stories of Steubenville.

On October 19, 1932, New York governor and presidential hopeful Franklin Roosevelt made an unscheduled stop in Weirton on his way to Wheeling. Roosevelt was in a yellow convertible, and when news of his motorcade reached Weirton, people turned out see him. My grandmother Lois Carpini remembers waiting by the window of her Weirton Heights home for FDR and can vividly recall the motorcade as it descended Pennsylvania Avenue on its way downtown. Roosevelt stopped at a vacant lot, soon to be

Supporters rally in Steubenville to cheer vice-presidential candidate Richard Nixon, who was running with Dwight Eisenhower during the presidential election of 1952. *Weirton Area Museum and Cultural Center.*

the post office on the corner of West Street and Mildren Avenue, and gave a short speech. Roosevelt became the first presidential candidate to campaign in the area. On October 7, 1952, Richard Nixon, although not running for president himself, visited Steubenville by train as the running mate for presidential hopeful Dwight Eisenhower.

During the 1960 election, West Virginia was a battleground state, and John F. Kennedy spent considerable time campaigning there. On May 1, 1960, he spoke in the lobby of Weirton's Millsop Community Center. A bust of Kennedy commemorates his visit in the room, unveiled by his brother Bobby Kennedy during his visit there in November 1965. Jimmy Carter was the next to visit, becoming the first sitting president to visit our area. Carter spoke at Steubenville High School on September 12, 1979. Reagan also campaigned here in October 1980, speaking at the Ohio Valley Towers in Steubenville. Finally, Bill Clinton campaigned in Weirton in July 1992, speaking in the community center as Kennedy had over thirty years before.

While in Steubenville, Lincoln said of his election as president, "If I adopt a wrong policy, the opportunity for condemnation will occur in four years. Then, I can be turned out and a better man with better views put in my place." That is the beauty of our government, and it is as true today as it was in 1861. The power is with the people.

THE CIVIL WAR

In our area, the Civil War was not fought as it was, for example, in Virginia or in Pennsylvania—not including Morgan's Raid, of course. We in this area were spared the big battles on our soil. But that doesn't mean that the war did not impact us. In Hancock County, 466 men went to fight in the Civil War. In addition, the home guard organized as the Panhandle Greys in Hancock County consisted of 59 men at its height in 1862. But it was one Holliday's Cove native, James Andrews, who made quite an impact during the Civil War. James was born here in the Cove in 1829, and after living quite a colorful life as a teacher, brickmaker and housepainter, among other professions, ended up in Kentucky at the outbreak of the war. Jack Welch, in his book *The History of Hancock County*, explains that during a trip to Louisville, Andrews was "contacted by a Northern officer who suggested he become a spy for the Union. He was a strong Union sympathizer, though he did profess to be a Secessionist." After many successful trips south selling needed medical supplies, Andrews gained access to Southern military positions and,

View of Steubenville's Market Street looking west between Third and Fourth Streets.
Jefferson County Historical Association.

upon his return to the Northern lines, would report to Union officials of all he learned.

By April 1862, Andrews had been chosen to lead a group of twenty-two men from the Second, Twenty-First and Thirty-Third Ohio Volunteer Infantry to travel to Marietta, Georgia, and capture a locomotive called the General and bring it north, burning bridges and disrupting rail lines as they made their way to the Union lines. Though group did succeed in capturing the locomotive, the mission ultimately failed—but not before an exciting and daring attempt by Andrews and his men to move the locomotive north. In 1956, Walt Disney memorialized the event in his movie *The Great Locomotive*

Chase, staring Fess Parker. Andrews never returned to Holliday's Cove. He was captured and hanged by the Confederacy for treason on June 7, 1862. You can still visit the General today, as it is permanently parked in the Southern Museum of Civil War and Locomotive History in Kennesaw, Georgia. Coincidentally enough, one of Andrews's men who took an active role in the operation to capture the locomotive was William Pittenger, a native of Jefferson County, Ohio. Due to his bravery during the raid, Pittenger received the fifth Medal of Honor ever to be awarded in United States history.

In Jefferson County, thousands of soldiers fought for the Union during the Civil War. According to the *1897 Centennial Souvenir of Steubenville and Jefferson County*, twenty companies were organized in Steubenville and Jefferson County, in addition to Jefferson County soldiers who served in forty-five other companies. Jefferson County has an impressive war record, to be sure, and it is said that there was "not a battle fought of any importance in which some of Jefferson county's sons did not take part." But the efforts of those on home front were also of great importance.

One of my favorite stories about Steubenville during the Civil War years is that of the sending off of the first group of Steubenville soldiers, a short time after Abraham Lincoln called on seventy-five thousand volunteers to march south and squash the rebellion. The excitement of that specific time and place in Steubenville was captured by Emelda Junkin Donaldson in her address to the Fort Steuben Daughters of the American Revolution in 1922, at a dinner at the Fort Steuben Hotel. Donaldson was, at the time of the address, eighty-one years old and had lived and experienced the Civil War in Steubenville firsthand. Addressing the crowd, Donaldson related how the old bell on the top of the courthouse rang to muster the townsfolk to enlist. That bell today is in Union Cemetery. The prominent ladies in town also wanted to show their support for the war effort and soon formed the Woman's Soldiers Aid Society. The society's first office was located on Market Street east of where the fountain at Fort Steuben Park is located today. Upon the disembarkation of the first wave of soldiers from Steubenville, amid the parade of soldiers and civilians marching down Market Street to the station at the foot of the hill, the soldiers stopped at the Woman's Soldiers Aid Society. Here, speeches were made, and a handsome flag furnished by the society was given to the men, in addition to a Bible from a Mrs. Beatty on behalf of the Bible Society. Little did the soldiers know that the war would last almost four more years from that moment on.

Not unlike their descendants during World War II, the Woman's Soldiers Aid Society did its part to help the war effort. Uniforms and clothing were

Mid-nineteenth-century view of West Market Street in Steubenville. *Jefferson County Historical Association.*

made by the group to aid the soldiers, and due to the fact that at that time, Steubenville was a center for woolen manufacturing, supplies were readily on hand. Jellies and fruits were saved in case there was need. The ladies helped the families of those soldiers in the service who were in need, helping them to secure jobs and write letters and generally advising the families in solving perplexing questions. Donaldson waxes warmly of the efforts of

Steubenville folk during the Civil War, and her address is worth the read. One can find it preserved for posterity on the Jefferson County Historical Association's website.

The Civil War, although long over, was and continues to be a nationally defining event in our history. The struggles our ancestors endured in fighting that fight can no longer be passed down in their own words by the living—except by the objects they left behind. Lewis Anile, a local historian and collector, sums it up powerfully in this quote about history: "It has been said that history is a way to live extra lives, to cheat the limits of flesh and blood, to roll the rock back from the tomb and free the resurrected dead." The Civil War still speaks to us of the past.

THE COST OF FREEDOM

Recently, my wife and I watched a fascinating documentary titled *They Shall Not Grow Old*. This documentary, directed by Peter Jackson, used over six hundred hours of interviews with World War I veterans and over one thousand hours of film from the Imperial War Museum in London to tell the stories of British soldiers fighting in World War I. The most fascinating part about the whole program is that Jackson's studio colorized and sharpened the one-hundred-year-old film, which gives the viewer a totally new perspective and appreciation of what fighting was like during the Great War. It was terrible what the soldiers endured, and the color images make it come to life in a way black-and-white film lacks. The title is appropriate, coming from a poem written in 1914 by Laurence Binyon titled "For the Fallen." It's worth the read. We certainly owe much to those who went off to fight for our county, and we especially honor those who gave, in Lincoln's words, "the last full measure of devotion."

Named for Revolutionary War veteran Baron von Steuben, a Prussian soldier who helped the American cause for independence, Steubenville has sent troops to aid in all American conflicts since the War of 1812. Colonel Tappan led a company of troops from Steubenville to meet British and Indian forces engaged near Sandusky. During the Mexican-American War in 1846, the Steubenville Greys marched south, and many Steubenville sons fought with distinction during the Civil War. During World War I, 1,400 men from Steubenville fought in the conflict. Among these, Captain Francis McCook, a Steubenville native, was wounded in September 1918 and later passed on while encouraging his men during a barrage by enemy shot and shell. Captain McCook is buried in France. Other World War I soldiers from Steubenville killed include Corporal Howard Preble and Private Sylvester Berney, who both lost their lives in France in September and October 1918, respectively. In July 1921, both men's remains, along with those of another Jefferson County veteran, were returned to the city to a hero's welcome.

During World War II in Steubenville and Jefferson County, over twelve thousand soldiers went to war, many of whom never returned. One of the first was Julius Young, a seaman first class, who was killed in action in the Pacific in 1942. Sergeant Thomas Moxley Jr. was killed when his glider collided with another over New Mexico in 1942. Jerome Edwards, a Tuskegee Airman, paid the ultimate sacrifice for our country in May 1943 when his plane malfunctioned stateside. On April 30, 1944, an honor roll was erected in front of the courthouse on Market Street that listed the soldiers from the county who served and those who paid the ultimate sacrifice. That structure is no longer standing, having been removed due to deterioration, but a mural depicting it is located on Market Street. The mural was completed in 1995.

In Hancock County, 4,356 soldiers joined the service in World War II, including 82 women. From Weirton Steel alone, not bound by county or state lines, over 5,000 employees went to war, and 115 never returned. To honor their legacy, the Weirton Steel Employees Honor Roll was erected on the corner of Main Street and Pennsylvania Avenue in 1944. It was

A 1950s photograph of the Weirton Steel Employees Honor Roll from World War II located at the corner of Pennsylvania Avenue and Main Street. *Weirton Area Museum and Cultural Center.*

Postcard view of the Jefferson County Honor Roll located on the grounds of the county courthouse in Steubenville. *Author's collection.*

removed in 1959, and a new brick edifice was built in 1990 near the former site of the Weirton Steel General Office. The eagle that adorned the original structure can be seen today in the Weirton Museum. Also, on Veterans Day 1959, another beautiful war memorial was dedicated in front of the Millsop Community Center amid huge crowds.

There are many other memorials dedicated to the fallen in our area. One of my favorites is the large marble memorial in Union Cemetery dedicated on May 30, 1869, to the soldiers and sailors of Jefferson County who fought in the Civil War. But erecting a monument will never be enough to honor those who paid the supreme sacrifice. We must also remember the many brave soldiers who gave their lives fighting in Korea, Vietnam and our more recent conflicts. The cost of freedom is heavy.

Every day, not just on Memorial Day, we should, amid the sunny weather, family picnics and barbecues, remember the fallen who gave it all and those who never came home. As Laurence Binyon wrote,

> *They shall grow not old, as we that are left grow old;*
> *Age shall not weary them, nor the years condemn.*
> *At the going down of the sun and in the morning,*
> *We will remember them.*

Chapter 6

CHILLING STORIES

*H*alloween is a very special time for us in the Ohio Valley. We seek out spooky, chilling or scary things that we don't typically go for at other times of year. Some people like to be scared by movies or walk through haunted houses; as for me, I get a chill from stories of our past. As a historian, I find that true events often are stranger than fiction. That is how some ghost stories are started, after all. A true event makes a good story, which develops into an even better ghost story. The following three stories are true events and could be told as such tales. I find the ghosts of our historic past are often scarier than the ghouls we invent on our own.

Steubenville is old, and as in any old town, there was once a town center. Our town center was on Market Street between Fourth and Third Streets. The courthouse, the third to be built on that site, was the center of town, and the green space directly across the street was the city market square. In the early nineteenth century, that green space also served as the site of Steubenville's whipping post. It seems that whippings took place there on a regular basis. The last one occurred around 1810. A shopkeeper who owned a business on Market Street stole some goods from Bezaleel Wells. The shopkeeper was tried, found guilty and sentenced to pay fines, serve jail time and be whipped nine times on his bare back with a cat-o'-nine-tails. Although that is one of the more prominent stories of a whipping that took place in the market square, one could assume that this site witnessed many others in its history.

According to local lore, around the same spot, during the 1820s, a gentleman called Peter Snyder was digging a well along Third Street just

Construction of the Jefferson County Courthouse. This building was the third courthouse to occupy the site and was completed in 1874. *Jefferson County Historical Association.*

south of Market Street. When Peter reached one hundred feet deep, the well collapsed, entombing Mr. Snyder inside. His remains were never recovered. The story has been passed down through the years, showing up in local history books in 1897 and 1947. The story is plausible, due to the fact that the primitive water system, set up in the early years of Steubenville with wooden pipes and powered by natural springs, failed around this time. It wasn't until around 1836 that a pumping house was erected along the river just south of the Market Street Bridge.

Just across Market Street from the green space is the elegant Jefferson County Courthouse. This building, erected in 1874, was described at the time as one of the most beautiful in Ohio. It has undergone some changes since then, most notably the removal of the bell tower and the mansard roof. It was from one of the upper-story windows that Mrs. Julia Petrosky decided to jump on June 20, 1917, after being found guilty of murder. Mrs. Petrosky had fallen in love with Sheriff George Huscroft, and when she went to visit Huscroft at his office, Mr. Beem, the county jail trustee, denied her entry. She pulled out a gun and shot Beem. Julia was sure she would be found innocent, but it was not to be, and when the guilty verdict was handed down, Julia went for the windows and jumped to her death, landing on the steps below.

History is all around us, and it is not always pleasant to remember. There are stories to be told of the places we live that would chill us to the bone. The facts are scary on their own, with no need to embellish them. And if one is looking for a ghost, there are plenty of stories that could serve as inspiration. A poor soul whipped at the whipping post, a lost worker digging a well or a distraught woman looking for justice—all can be found along Market Street in beautiful and historic downtown Steubenville.

A Frightful Past

Over the years, I have tried as best I could to find as many ghost stories or spooky stories as possible that took place in our area, but there aren't many. It seems that our spirits passed peacefully into the beyond and didn't stick around to bother the living too much.

Ghosts, on the other hand, don't necessarily always need to be the traditional kind—deceased folks who haunt us—but rather just the memory of a specific event or thing. That is why visitors to battlefields sometime have strong emotional reactions to the space. It is not that there are ghosts floating around, but rather that the memory of what transpired there is overwhelming. Unfortunately, these strong memories are typically connected with traumatic events. Looking at our area's past, there are certainly many stories that would be the basis for a ghost story. And not only that, but we can also base our stories on historical facts to back them up. Typically, ghost stories don't have much truth to verify their historical accuracy.

A tragic story that always fascinated me, since I grew up near the site of the event, could certainly be the basis of a ghost story, and it goes back to our early history in this area. The story begins in the early 1780s; the American Revolution was winding down in the East, but on the western frontier, things were beginning to heat up. This wasn't necessarily due to British troops waging war, in the fashion of the eastern battles, but many of their Native American allies were continuing to wage war on the American settlers on the eastern shore of the Ohio River in the form of raids. The history of the Native Americans' role in the American Revolution is complex and one that is varied depending on the particular tribe in question. War parties were formed on both the settler and Native sides, and deadly attacks were common. In the spring of 1782, a settler named Thomas Campbell was gathering sap from his sugar maple trees near his home on Kings Creek, in the area where Country Club Estates in Weirton is now. Thomas had set up a sugar camp on the hill above his cabin and was working hard to provide syrup for his family. After a long day's work, Thomas returned to his log cabin on the creek exhausted, with one bucket of syrup. His wife, noticing his exhaustion, offered to return to the sugar camp to retrieve the second bucket if Thomas watched their child. As she traversed the terrain near the present site of Culler Road, reaching the top of the hill, she encountered a band of Native Americans traveling in the direction of her home. One of the Natives shot at her but missed. Mrs. Campbell ran to a neighboring homestead and alerted the community. At once, a band of settlers was formed and dispatched in the direction of the Campbell cabin. Upon arriving at the home on Kings Creek, they found Thomas slain, lying in the doorway with his flintlock nearby. The child had also been killed and was found near the cabin. Both were scalped, as was the custom of the Natives at that time. The war party was tracked by the settlers, but it were not found, and no revenge was waged on the Natives in retaliation for this attack. Certainly, atrocities were waged on both sides of the conflict in those days.

Another tragic story of our area occurred around 1846, when the threat of Native American war parties was a thing of the past. Holliday's Cove, a small but thriving community, was lucky to have a medical doctor in residence, and with his practice in the community, he was able to care for the local people. Dr. Darwin Stanton, brother of Secretary of War Edwin Stanton, was born in Steubenville in 1816 and graduated from the University of Pennsylvania in 1838. Edwin loved his younger brother and paid for his education. By 1846, though, Darwin, having served as assistant clerk of the

House of Representatives in Washington, D.C., returned to Holliday's Cove, as he was suffering from what was described then as "the fever." Darwin was housed in the community, in a residence that was located in Cove Commons near the site of the current Cove Presbyterian Church. Darwin was confined to an upper bedroom of the building. According to historian Mary Ferguson, "Darwin was real bad and his friends had been taking turns sitting up with him. That night, somehow, he got a needle he used for bleeding patients and took it with him to bed. The folks sitting here by his bed heard a dripping and thought the roof was leaking as it had rained earlier in the evening. By the time they got through looking for the leak, Darwin was dead. He had opened a vein in his leg and the blood had gone clear through the mattress onto the floor." When Edwin was notified of his brother's death, he quickly traveled to Holliday's Cove. He was so distraught that he wandered off into the woods around Holliday's Cove and disappeared for a time. After the death of Dr. Stanton, no one wanted to live in the old house, and it became a tavern for passing visitors operated by Mary Lyons. In the room where Dr. Darwin took his life was a bloodstain on the floor that would not come out. No matter how hard it was scrubbed, the stain remained as a reminder of the tragedy that took place in that room.

The log cabin of Thomas Campbell and the tavern are gone now, lost to history and progress. And although these tales are not ghost stories, their impact on the area can still be felt in the narratives they leave behind. Perhaps the next time you are near Kings Creek on a spring night, you may see in your mind's eye the cabin of Thomas Campbell or, while near Cove Commons, hear the faint dripping of blood from the bed of Dr. Stanton. Don't worry; these are just the ghosts of the past yearning to be remembered.

More Local Haunts

What is our fascination with stories from the past? I am talking not about the history we learn about in school but about stories we hear from our loved ones. Anecdotal and often personal, these stories connect us and help make the past not so distant. In museums, our goal is to tell the stories of the past, and we strive to do that by finding ways to connect them and make them relevant to visitors in the present. Like most folklore, ghost stories can be useful, too. I think primarily they are told to scare us, give us a chill or teach us something. For me, they are one more way we can connect to the past.

One of my favorite stories in this area is about the ghost that is said to walk the train tracks, now the Panhandle Trail in Colliers. Recorded by folklorist Ruth Ann Musick in her book *Coffin Hollow and Other Ghost Tales*, this apparition is that of an old man who was run over by a train between Colliers and Weirton. As the story goes, a family rented a home near the railroad tracks just outside of the town, and one night while sitting on their back porch, they saw a man walking along the tracks drinking from a brown paper bag. He then sat down on the tracks, apparently unaware that a train was fast approaching. One of the residents of the house, who was witnessing all of this from a distance, began to run across the long lawn toward the tracks, yelling for the old man to move off the tracks. He was too late, and the steam engine roared swiftly past. After the train had departed, expecting to see a gruesome scene, the spectator was met with nothing that indicated anyone was ever there. The man, confused, returned to his house, telling his wife—who had seen the old man, too—that the tracks were empty. Later, he found out that years before, there was indeed a stranger in Colliers who was killed on the tracks after the townsfolk ran him out of town. After this incident, the ghost of the old man on the rails was never seen by the residents again. Whether or not this story is rooted in true events is unclear.

Another great ghost story in our area is about the ghost that is said to haunt the main branch of the Steubenville Public Library. In a 2016

Postcard view of the Carnegie Library in Steubenville. *Author's collection.*

article, Alan Hall, retired director of the library, recounted that when he arrived at the library in 1983, the staff asked him if he had been to the attic. Upon examination, he found the tower room where the very first library director had her office for a time, when the building was new. On the door was a poster indicating that here was the home of the library ghost. After some digging into the history of the building, Hall discovered that the resident ghost was most likely that of Ellen Summers Wilson, the first librarian. Wilson died tragically of tuberculosis in August 1904 at the age of thirty-one, after only two years as director. Alan tells me that if the ghost exists, it is friendly and happy to welcome visitors to the library. He also says that while Ellen was director, she created a special reading area for veterans of the Civil War. I agree with Alan's statement that perhaps the old veterans never left.

The story of our friendly librarian ghost is rooted in fact. Ellen Summers Wilson existed and met an untimely end. Another local story is not necessarily a ghost story, but sometimes fact is stranger than fiction. Historian Mary Ferguson, one of my favorite sources of local lore, tells the story of a local person who also met an untimely end. In the late fall of 1903, Zane Buchanan, a resident of Holliday's Cove, contracted the "black pox." Mary relates that when Zane died, his body was removed from the upstairs window of his home so as to not contaminate the first floor. She writes,

"They took him through town in the dead of night and the men, who carried him on the wagon, made room for a couple of jugs for sipping to ward off evil spirits and to keep them clear of the black pox." The undertakers claimed that when they arrived at Three Springs Cemetery, they buried Zane facedown, although this can't be proven. To bury someone facedown is an old medieval tradition originating in Europe during the time of the plagues. This practice was meant to ensure that the dead would not arise and infect the living with the disease. This obviously was the intent of the undertakers: to protect the living of Holliday's Cove.

Grave of Ensley Zane Buchanan located in Three Springs Cemetery in Weirton. *Author's collection.*

Chapter 7

COMMUNITY CELEBRATIONS AND CHALLENGES

*T*he history of our community is full of commemorations, anniversaries and celebrations. Commemorating the anniversary of a past event is what we historians live for. Take, for instance, the Civil War sesquicentennial that took place starting in 2011. Battlefields across the country were packed with events and programs commemorating the event, and that generally created a renewed interest in that specific aspect of American history. As many history enthusiasts may remember, that was also the response to the events held in the 1960s on the occasion of the conflict's centennial.

Here in Steubenville, we have a very long tradition of commemorations and celebrations over the years. Going way back, one of the very first extensive community commemorations in our city took place on the occasion of the centennial of the founding of Steubenville and Jefferson County in 1897. According to reports in the newspaper publications of the period, the event, which took place on August 24, 25 and 26, 1897, would be "the grandest event in the history of Steubenville and Jefferson County." The streets of Steubenville were decorated from top to bottom with decorations, flags, bunting and the like. The grandest of all the decorations were four large arches that spanned four of the city's main streets. The arches were also adorned with electric lights, and at night, they lit up the dark city. Additional decorations on the streets included portraits of famous personalities like Lincoln, Ulysses S. Grant and Baron von Steuben adorning available windows; included were local celebrities like Edwin Stanton, Bezaleel Wells

Photograph showing the centennial decorations at the intersection of Fourth and Market Streets in Steubenville, taken on July 4, 1876. *Jefferson County Historical Association.*

and James Ross, to name a few. A beautiful mural commemorating one of the arches was recently restored and is located today on the corner of Washington and North Fifth Streets across from Froehlich's Classic Corner.

A large crowd for the centennial events was expected, and by all accounts, these expectations were realized, with many thousands of visitors flooding the city. On the first day of the event, dedicated to Edwin Stanton, it was reported in the *Steubenville Herald* that "for more than two hours the streets in the vicinity of Fourth and Market and the public square were almost impassable for people and the scene was certainly an inspiring one." Later, the *Herald* estimated that over five thousand visitors arrived in town that day, noting that the Pan Handle Railroad would be "taxed to its utmost to handle the crowds." Attracting attention that evening, as well, was a huge bonfire that was intentionally set across the river on the West Virginia side opposite Market Street. At seven o'clock that first evening, a crowd of several hundred assembled on South Third Street, below Market Street, for a grand bicycle and lantern parade led by Bueche's Band, encompassing many of the principal streets in the city.

Arriving with the crowds the night before, Civil War general Daniel Sickles steamed into Steubenville to be met by a crowd of over one thousand visitors gathered for his late-night arrival. It was reported that "no man, not excepting any of the Presidents, even received a heartier welcome to Steubenville than did the gallant old soldier." There were other dignitaries in town, as well, but none as popular as General Sickles, who lost a leg at Gettysburg and was a close personal friend of Edwin Stanton.

Over the three days of the festivities, there were parties, meetings, luncheons and receptions, followed by the grand parade, which hosted floats, community representatives, Civil War veterans and soldiers—who were encamped on the hilltop of Pleasant Heights—among many others. Photographs of this parade do exist, and some are included in the book *Images of America: Steubenville* by Sandy Day and Alan Hall, along with many other images of the grand centennial in Steubenville.

The 1897 event is fairly well documented; numerous newspaper accounts and primary sources recounted the events. One source I use often in researching historic Steubenville is the 1897 book titled *Centennial Souvenir of Steubenville and Jefferson County*. According to newspaper accounts, the book was available for purchase at the event. "It is the big blue book containing a complete history of Jefferson County and six hundred pictures of pretty views, handsome buildings, fine streets etc. just the thing for every visitor to take home with them." Books were available from street vendors, newsdealers, the U.S. Hotel and Filson and Son Studios and at the office of the Herald Publishing Company. Production was reportedly limited, although a good number of these books have survived the years.

Wooden nickel souvenir from the 1947 Steubenville sesquicentennial. *Author's collection.*

Photograph showing a scene from the Steubenville centennial in August 1897. *Jerry Barilla.*

Today, over 125 years after the closing of the celebration, it could still be considered one of the biggest events held in our city's history. Although the focus of the festival was looking to the past, the centennial celebration could be viewed as an important moment in time in our community's history depicting the importance of all those who came before and what was valuable to those in 1897. Their pride in our community was evident, and their pride lives on today in their contribution to the history of our region.

The Big Snow of 1950

Certain events in the life of a community seem to stick around. On a national scale, I think that is common. For my grandparents, it was remembering where they were on December 7, 1941, when the Japanese attacked Pearl Harbor. For my parents, it was when JFK was assassinated in November 1963. For my generation, it was the terrorist attacks of September 11, 2001. Significant events like this seem to live on in our collective memory.

Here in our valley, one such event that has transcended time is the 1950 Thanksgiving snowstorm.

November 2020 marked the seventieth anniversary of this epic storm. Growing up here, it was always something that was talked about among my grandparents' generation. That week, the snow began on Thanksgiving and continued to fall, unrelenting, through the weekend, dumping several feet of snow on our valley. Nationally, it was called the Great Appalachian Storm of 1950, and it is still studied today as a superstorm. It is listed as a category 5 Extreme Level storm on the Regional Snowfall Index compiled by the National Oceanic and Atmospheric Administration's National Centers for Environmental Information. According to their website for the Ohio Valley region, which encompasses the states of West Virginia, Ohio, Indiana, Kentucky, Tennessee, Illinois and Missouri, the snowstorm was the "worst storm to impact the Ohio Valley." The website explains that the second-worst storm occurred in March 1993, but the 1950 storm was one of only four category 5 storms that have hit this region since 1900.

In Steubenville, WTOV 9 meteorologist Jeff Oechslein explained in a 2015 report that the snowfall was a record, totaling forty-one inches of snow. Although reports vary, documentation of up to forty-four inches in some places does exist. Memories vary of the actual amount of snow that fell from town to town, but there was a lot of it. The *Steubenville Herald Star* recorded at the time that roads were completely impassable and some were blocked by drifts of snow up to twenty-five feet in places. The weight of the snow was enormous—so much so that the mansard roof of the Jefferson County Courthouse collapsed under the weight. It was reported that "more than one third of the roof and fourth floor of the courthouse crashed into No. 1 Courtroom." The county law library was completely wrecked, as were many county records. With the collapse came the additional danger of the rest of the 1874 structure coming down as well. The ceilings of the offices directly below the debris sagged, too—in some places up to eight inches. The damage was valued at around $200,000. Today, if you look at the top floor of the courthouse, you can clearly see the repair to the building. To mitigate the danger at the Hub department store, the male employees were pressed into service to go to the roof and shovel the snow off. The Steubenville Christmas parade, which was scheduled for November 25, was postponed until December 8, as recounted by the *Herald Star*. Evidently, Santa, who makes a regular appearance even up to the present during the festivities, wired the city and explained he was snowbound in Harrisburg, Pennsylvania.

View from the overhead bridge on Weirton Steel during the Thanksgiving snowstorm of 1950. *Weirton Area Museum and Cultural Center.*

The newly created city of Weirton was beside itself in the job of digging out. Bulldozers were dispatched from Weirton Steel and Starvaggi Industries to help clear the roads. Mike Starvaggi, owner of the P&W Bus Company, was touted as a hero in keeping his buses running between Weirton and Steubenville. It was important to keep the avenues of transportation open to resupply stores with necessities. One important necessity was milk. Dennis Jones, in his book *Images of America: Weirton*—which is still available and has a whole chapter dedicated to the "Perfect Storm," complete with pictures of the event—recalls that Weirton Steel employees loaded and transported 1,200 gallons of milk in company trucks to the Weir-Cove Dairy for bottling and distribution. Without this emergency shipment of milk, Steubenville and Weirton would have experienced an extended shortage. The trucks with chains on their tires continued delivering despite the weather.

What I enjoy most about this event is the stories people have of their experiences in the blizzard. One of my favorites is the story the late David Weir related to the Weirton Museum about the blizzard. David and his family were staying at the Lodge, their home next to Williams Country Club. He relates that they were pretty well stocked with provisions, but one evening, a man arrived at the residence in a military snowsuit carrying a rucksack full of food. It turned out to be Tom Millsop, who had trekked through the deep snow from his home thinking that the Weir family was in need. As David writes, "It had taken him nearly all day. Tom was an old marine and wasn't going to let something like a little snow stop him." But the best part about David's experience was sledding with his grandmother in the following days, making memories that lasted a lifetime in the "Big Snow."

For area children, this snowstorm resulted in the cancelation of school for a week. Naturally, most kids spent their time off sledding on the freshly cleared and icy roads, which proved to be the perfect readymade sled-riding tracks. Steubenville mayor Jerry Barilla remembered that the streets were the best places to ride in Steubenville. Not as many folks had cars then, and Jerry recalled that Adams Street Hill and South Street Hill were the best places to ride in those days. Howard Street was also a popular place in Weirton to sled ride due to its steepness crossing Weir Avenue down to the Mill. Brightway on Marland Heights was also quite the ride. George Bilderback, a resident of Heazlett Avenue at that time, recounted to the Weirton Museum that after

Cars covered in snow near Steelworks Gate No. 1 and the Weirton Bus Terminal. *Weirton Area Museum and Cultural Center.*

a Weirton Steel bulldozer plowed the street and the snow was packed down, the neighborhood kids used that hill for sledding, too. Each neighborhood had its own place for sledding that was the best.

The 1950 Thanksgiving snowstorm was one to remember. And if you are privileged enough to remember back over seventy years to that weekend, chances are you have a story to tell. I would encourage you to tell your loved ones about waking up and looking out the window on a once-in-a-lifetime event. I'll bet you'll remember the cold weather, but the memories you made will keep you warm for years to come.

CHRISTMAS IN STEUBENVILLE

It seems to many that nowadays, the Christmas holiday season starts earlier, has become overcommercialized and overtaxes the finances. And that all may be true, but only if you let it be so. Historically speaking, Christmas celebrations in the past were much simpler in material goods, but the spirit of Christmas was very much alive.

It is often asked of me what Christmas at Historic Fort Steuben was like for the First American Regiment, which was stationed here in 1786. We know that in December that year, there were frigid temperatures and snow—lots of it. The fort was well supplied with whiskey, turkey, venison, bear, racoon and panther that holiday. Probably, the occasion was not marked, other than by a little extra rations for the day. The business of just surviving in the remote outpost was first and foremost in the minds of the soldiers stationed here. That Christmas was the first on record in Steubenville.

Christmas in Steubenville in 1830 was more of a festive affair compared to the one at the fort forty-four years earlier. According to an article published in the *Steubenville Evening Star* in 1890 about Christmas sixty years previously, the festivities were different but full of cheer. Christmas gifts were exchanged, but most presents to children were a "cake, a penny, a sixpence, or some sweetmeat." The children would fire muskets and makeshift cannons in the air in celebration of the holiday, so much so that "the very air was redolent with the smell of burnt powder." Most men did not work and generally stayed home with their families and friends. The Christmas meal was not just turkey but also deer, bear and other game. Most of the holiday celebrations for the working-class folk were held at the hotels or taverns in the city. Here, they would have a strong drink, play a game of shinny (a hockey-like game) or engage in a shooting match. According to the article, the best sport of the day was catching a greased pig. A razorback pig was shaved and greased, and whoever caught it got to keep it.

For the "nobility" of Steubenville, Christmas meant sleigh rides to a neighboring town's tavern or hotel for a festive holiday evening. Excursions went out to Wellsburg, Brilliant or to the Forks for an evening of fun. Revelers riding in a sleigh holding eight to twelve people would arrive to a lavish supper and a punch bowl filled with a hot toddy that took the chill off. Then the festivities began. They would dance the Virginia Reel and other dances popular in those days to the music of a single violin. No visits by our jolly old friend were mentioned.

It's argued by historians that our particular image of Santa comes from the poem "A Visit from St. Nicholas," also known as "'Twas the Night Before Christmas." The author, Clement Moore, published the work in 1823 in a Troy, New York newspaper. The earliest account I can find in our area of the publication of the poem appeared in the *Wheeling Daily Times* on January 4, 1843. The poem was changed from expecting Santa on Christmas to New Years' Eve in that publication. Another Christmas classic that was known in our area was Charles Dickens's short story "A Christmas Carol," published in 1843. By 1844, there were advertisements from various booksellers in our region that promoted the story.

In the 1860s, during the height of the Civil War, Christmas went on as it always had in Steubenville. And although the Christmas tree was not unknown in these parts at that time, most decorations were simply described as evergreens. During Christmas in 1863, Steubenville's Ladies Soldiers Aid Society held a Christmas festival taking advantage of the "homemade" skills of the prominent members of Steubenville society. The evergreen decorated the hall, and the ladies decorated tables with their crafts. For the aid of the Union soldiers, the group raised over $1,000, a large sum at that time. The following Christmas, 1864, brought a gift to the nation, as recorded in the *Steubenville Weekly Herald*. On December 28, it was reported that General Sherman presented the captured city of Savannah to the American people as a Christmas gift, including "800 rebel prisoners, 150 great guns, 130 locomotives and 190 cars, 3 steamers, several blown up iron clads and 33,000 bales of cotton." That was the last Christmas of the war.

In 1867, there was a lovely description of Christmas in Steubenville encompassed in the *Steubenville Weekly Herald*. Shops were open on Christmas Eve to give shoppers an opportunity to get their last-minute gifts. "The interior of very many of the city residences were gratefully decorated with evergreens, and in many a home, children danced about the Christmas tree which Santa

Claus had hung over with gifts for their especial delight." It seems that by this time in Steubenville, the Christmas tree had arrived for domestic use.

By June 1870, Christmas became a national holiday. And the *Steubenville Weekly Herald* summed it up: "No day in the year is so eagerly looked forward to by all classes and conditions of people. So far from its commemoration becoming less marked as the years roll on, each succeeding recurrence of the feast seems to be still more generally observed than the last, and from all indications to-day will form no exception to the rule." Christmas seemed to them to grow with each passing year.

Looking back, it seems that Christmas past was a time of simple gifts, decorations and family. Christmas still comes despite all the troubles in the world. The promises and hopes that our ancestors celebrated are still true today. A simple Christmas is not so bad; let us reflect on our past and hope for the future.

Christmas Morning

Waking up on Christmas morning in my house is always an exciting affair. The magic begins the night before when each one of my children hangs their stocking on the mantel with care. Each of their stockings were handmade with love by my wife. Getting them to go to bed is the real trick because, like most kids, they are excited that soon Santa will be stopping by our house to deliver their presents. I make sure to mail their lists to the North Pole early, so Santa has plenty of time to prepare. Milk and cookies are, naturally, always ready for Santa, in addition to a few carrots for the reindeer. We had to apologize to Santa one year, as one of my twins got up early on Christmas morning and helped himself to the cookies and milk before Santa had a chance to enjoy them. Naturally, the carrots were left untouched. Despite this, he was still on the nice list.

On Christmas morning, my children rush to the living room to see what has been left for them. It is one of the best feelings to see the smiles and joy and hear the cries of delight as they tear open their presents. I remember well that feeling as a child. Now, I get to relive it with my children. Typically, among the piles of stuff from Santa are the small few gifts that are given by my wife and me to our children and to each other. In my opinion, those are the best gifts, because they are the ones that are given with the most loving intent. They show that you care and have thought of the person, no matter how big or small the gift is.

Finding that perfect gift, though, can sometimes be a challenge. In our current day and age, we have the convenience of ordering pretty much anything online without leaving our home. This benefits me since I work, and I can't always go out shopping. Without online sales, I would be sunk. In the not-too-distant past, though, we didn't have the computer to fall back on. We had to put some effort into finding that perfect gift. One could order from a catalogue, but if the place you were shopping didn't have it, you didn't get it.

In our town over the years, there were many options as to where to shop. Traditionally, a good business would always advertise Christmas sales in December, and that is evident going back as far as I could go in the paper. In December 1865, Steubenville residents could stop at William Dougherty's for "choice dry goods for the holidays, at the corner of 3rd and Market. Goods brought expressly for the holidays. Bargains will be given in Christmas and New Years presents." Or one could go over to the "Boston Bulletin" store, where, it was advertised in December 1865, the whole stock was marked down. Many deals could be had, such as balmoral skirts, "now at $1 a skirt"; hoopskirts were reduced; and hosiery, cloaks and the finest imported kid gloves were all possible gifts.

By the later part of the nineteenth century, choices to shop for presents had expanded quite a bit in Steubenville. A popular location in town was Sulzbacher's Department Store, located on the corner of Market and Court Alley in the Cochrane Building. Today, that site is home to the old Demarks Building, currently the Antique Warehouse. According to Steubenville's 1897 centennial book, Sulzbacher's store occupied three floors and a basement filled with merchandise. House furnishings were in the basement, followed by the dry goods and notion departments on the first. The second floor held the millinery and the cloak and ladies' readymade wear department, and on the third was the millinery workroom. Just like most stores, Sulzbacher's advertised Christmas deals. On December 4, 1896, the *Steubenville Herald* ran an advertisement that stated, "Ready for Christmas. Now is the time to buy. Don't wait. You avoid the crowds and get first choice. Our stock of goods all in for the holidays. The supplies for Santa Clause are in the basement." Starting to advertise early was the key. For the young folks, Sulzbacher's had toys, especially dolls. That same year, 1896, Sulzbacher's advertised dolls that were imported especially for sale at the shop. These dolls, according to the advertisement, had bisque heads, closing eyes and natural wigs—all for twenty-five cents. They also carried a complete line of iron toys, a toy Bissell carpet sweeper and building blocks, all for under one dollar.

Winter view of Market Street west from Fourth Street taken in 1874. *Jefferson County Historical Association.*

Sulzbacher's had to be competitive, because there were plenty of other department stores in Steubenville. Directly across Market Square, now the green space next to the city building, on the corner of Market and South Third Streets, stood the impressive Munker's Store. This building would have stood where the fountain is in Fort Steuben Park today. According to the 1897 centennial book, in 1892, Jones Munker constructed "the finest business building in the city. The building is three story and basement….92 feet on Market Street, and 33 feet on Third. The basement is 9 feet high, first floor 17 feet, second floor 14 feet, and third floor 12 feet." This was a massive building, and surviving pictures from the time confirm that it was a unique structure. The store was laid out similarly to Sulzbacher's. Domestic goods were in the basement, as well as trunks. The first floor held boys' and children's clothing, gents' furnishings goods and the hat and cap department. The second floor was men's readymade clothing and the merchant tailoring department. The ladies' department was located in another part of the building and was stocked with cloaks, dry goods, hosiery, readymade wear, silks, laces and fancy goods.

The fact that these two massive stores carrying similar goods could be supported by our city for decades is pretty impressive. There were many other stores in our community sprouting up that would be important to our history, too, at the same time that Munker's and Sulzbacher's were in business, like the Hub. No matter where you shopped, you were supporting a local business.

Ultimately, though, Christmas is more than gifts or department stores. It is more than a day off from work or a good dinner. It is a time to spend with family and be thankful for all the blessings we have been given over the year. For me, it is the joy in my children's faces when they tear open their presents on Christmas morning. But the greatest gift of all is the one that was given to all of us in the little town of Bethlehem, two thousand years ago. And that is the true reason of the season.

BIBLIOGRAPHY

Published Primary Sources

Hargest, Lloyd W. *To the Unsung Heroes of the Production Front*. Hargest & Steffen, 1950.

Pandelios, John George. *Memoirs of North Weirton 1920 through the 1930s*. Weirton Area Museum and Cultural Center, 2012.

Truax, Lewis. "The 200th Anniversary of the City of Weirton, West Va., and My Life Story as I Have Seen Weirton Grow." Unpublished manuscript in author's possession. Weirton, WV: 1971.

Published Secondary Sources

All Saints Greek Orthodox Church. *2017 Centennial Album*. Weirton, WV: All Saints Greek Orthodox Church, 2017.

Andrews, J.H. *Centennial Souvenir of Steubenville and Jefferson County, Ohio, 1797–1897*. Steubenville, OH: Herald, 1897.

Caldwell, J.A. *History of Belmont and Jefferson Counties, Ohio*. Wheeling, WV: Historical Publications, 1880.

Cramer, Zadok. *The Ohio and Mississippi Navigator*. Pittsburgh, PA: John Scull, 1802.

Day, Sandy, and Alan Hall, eds. *Steubenville Bicentennial, 1797–1997*. Apollo, PA: Closson Press, 1997.

Doyle, Joseph B. *Twentieth Century History of Steubenville and Jefferson County, Ohio.* Chicago: Richmond-Arnold, 1910.

Ferguson, Mary Shakley. *The History of Hollidays Cove.* Weirton, WV: Hancock County Sheltered Workshop, 1976.

———. "Christmas Memories" *Goldenseal* (January–March 1976): 14–18.

Holmes, John R. *Remembering Steubenville from Frontier Fort to Steel Valley.* Charleston, SC: The History Press, 2009.

———. *The Story of Fort Steuben.* Steubenville, OH: Fort Steuben Press, 2000.

Javersak, David. *History of Weirton, West Virginia.* Virginia Beach, VA: Donning, 1999.

Jones, Dennis. *Weirton: A Pageant of Nations.* Weirton, WV: Weirton Area Museum and Cultural Center, 2009.

Kraina, Jane, and Mary Zwierzchowski. "Death of a Gypsy King." *Goldenseal* (Winter 1998): 18–27.

Lanmon, Dwight P., comp. *Evaluating Your Collection: The 14 Points of Connoisseurship.* Winterthur, DE: Henry Francis du Pont Winterthur Museum, 1999.

Lindsey, Susan Carnahan. "Hancock County in World War II." Master's thesis, West Virginia University, 1949.

Musick, Ruth Ann. *Coffin Hollow and Other Ghost Tales.* Lexington: University Press of Kentucky, 1977.

Pietranton, Frank A. *History of Weirton and Holliday's Cove and Life of J.C. Williams.* Pittsburgh, PA: Pittsburgh Printing, 1936.

Sacred Heart of Mary Parish. *The Golden Anniversary Souvenir Album Commemorating the Founding of Sacred Heart of Mary Parish.* Weirton, WV: 1961.

Smucker, Anna Egan. *No Star Night.* New York: Alfred A. Knopf, 1989.

Stahr, Walter. *Stanton.* New York: Simon & Schuster, 2017.

Steubenville Sesquicentennial, 1797–1947: Veteran's Homecoming: July 2–6, 1947. Steubenville, OH: H.C. Cook, 1947.

Vidas, Theresa L. *Sacred Heart of Mary Parish, 1911–2011, Celebrating 100 Years of Devotion and Service, Sto Lat.* Weirton, WV: Sacred Heart of Mary Parish, 2011.

Welsh, Jack. *History of Hancock County, Virginia and West Virginia.* Wheeling, WV: Wheeling Printing and Litho, 1963.

Zwierzchowski, Mary. "An Easter Tragedy: The Weirton Bus Crash of 1951." *Goldenseal* (Spring 2004): 26–33.

Websites

Ancestry.com. www.ancestry.com.

The East Steubenville Site: West Virginia's Panhandle Archaic Culture. "Project Background." Last modified January 1, 2006. http://129.71.204.160/shpo/es/project.html.

Journals of the Lewis and Clark Expedition Online. "Journals." Accessed July 2022. https://lewisandclarkjournals.unl.edu/journals.

Library of Congress. Accessed July 2022. https://www.loc.gov/.

Meadowcroft Rockshelter and Historic Village. "About Us." Accessed July 2022. https://www.heinzhistorycenter.org/visit/.

Monge, Janet, and Emily S. Renschler. "The Samuel George Morton Cranial Collection: Historical Significance and New Research." *Expedition* 50, no. 3 (2008): 30–38. https://www.penn.museum/sites/expedition/the-samuel-george-morton-cranial-collection/.

Monticello. "The Louisiana Purchase." Accessed July 2022. https://www.monticello.org/thomas-jefferson/louisiana-lewis-clark/the-louisiana-purchase/.

Morton, Samuel George. *Crania Americana.* Philadelphia: John Penington, 1839. Retrieved from https://books.google.com/books?id=VX5PAQAAMAAJ&dq=morton+to+tappan+skulls&source=gbs_navlinks_s.

NewspaperArchive. www.newspaperarchive.com.

Stamp, Jimmy. "A Brief History of the Baseball." *Smithsonian Magazine* (June 28, 2013). https://www.smithsonianmag.com/arts-culture/a-brief-history-of-the-baseball-3685086/.

U.S. Department of the Interior: Bureau of Land Management. https://www.blm.gov/.

Virginia Center for Digital History. "Sergeant Patrick Gass." http://www2.vcdh.virginia.edu/lewisandclark/biddle/biographies_html/gass.html.

The West Virginia Encyclopedia. https://www.wvencyclopedia.org/.

ABOUT THE AUTHOR

Paul Zuros was born and raised in Weirton, West Virginia. Raised by parents who were interested in history, Paul developed his love for the past early on. His interest in local history started when he volunteered with the Hancock County Museum in New Cumberland and then later with the Weirton Area Museum and Cultural Center.

Paul graduated from Weir High School and went on to West Virginia University (WVU) to pursue a bachelor's degree in history and minor in public relations and Italian studies. While at WVU, he worked for the National Park Service in Richmond, Virginia, at the city's Civil War sites. Paul graduated from Duquesne University in Pittsburgh with a master's degree in public history with a concentration in decorative arts. Over the years, Paul has worked at the John Heinz History Center in its library and archive, the Fort Pitt Museum and the Carnegie Museums of Pittsburgh. Before returning to the Ohio Valley to take the reins as director of Historic Fort Steuben, Paul was operations manager with the West Virginia Humanities Council and served as the executive director of the Historic Craik Patton House, a historic house museum, both in Charleston, West Virginia. Paul currently holds the position of county administrator for Hancock County, West Virginia. He resides in Weirton, West Virginia, with his wife, Abigail, and their four children, Paulie, Francis, Arthur and Stella.